Challenging Genders

Non-Binary Experiences of Those Assigned Female at Birth

Michael Eric Brown
Daywalker Burill

Contributors: Aitijhya Kar, Alyssa Hillary, Caden Rocker, Emil Eichelberger, Gyps Curmi, Jo Smiley, Kai Yves Avery, Lis Regula, Maxfield Sparrow, Morgan West, Moss Billman, Sam Lacovara, Sav, Sé Sullivan, Shalen Lowell, Trystan Craigo

Cover Art Image by Daywalker Burill.

Printed in the United States of America

Published by Boundless Endeavors, Inc.
2292 North West 82nd Ave #3525
Miami, FL 33198-1525
U.S.A.
www.boundlessendeavors.com

First Printing, 2018

Library of Congress Control Number: 2018904880

ISBN-13: 978-0-9968309-6-6 (Print)
ISBN-10: 0-9968309-6-0 (Print)
ISBN-13: 978-0-9968309-7-3 (Ebook)
ISBN-10: 0-9968309-7-9 (Ebook)

Includes bibliographical references.

Reviews

Personal life stories about gender matter tremendously, as a range of diverse voices, provide a broader understanding of truths. Brown and Burill's collection of autobiographical narratives further demonstrate that gender is a spectrum, not a binary and as necessary, serves to open a door closed for so long from open dialogue. The silencing and repression of people whose gender challenges the two-gender system have hindered the healthy development of individuals who transgress, as well as society's holistic understanding of gender as being much more than merely male or female. This long-overdue manuscript provides an essential foundation for those seeking answers about the diversity of gender we as humans exemplify and for those trying to find themselves reflected back in books.

Shaun-Adrián Choflá,
Ed.D. - Anti-Bias Educator and Scholar

As a lecturer on gender topics, as a human being, as a Transwoman, this book has taken me back in time as well as examine where we are in this moment, and reflect on what the future may be for us.

The very in-depth conveyance of terminology as well as peeling the onion to reach the myriad of gender expressions is something that the lay-person can grasp as well as a teaching tool for educators, lecturers, pediatricians and semi-professionals working in our various communities.

Even as a Transwoman, with everything I have learned and know, I find myself often struggling to keep up on the Gender-Binary conversation with descriptions that can be at first confusing and seemingly fluid themselves. But it is through the eyes of, and the stories told that it becomes crystal clear that even in the midst of pain and emotional trauma the need to simply be our authentic selves is paramount to our survival. And the need to be understood and accepted is paramount to all of us in our reach for an equitable place in our communities, and a future where gender matters less than Who we are.

The stories contained, where each makes clear the distinctions that set them apart and embarked them on journeys of self-discovery full of dysphoria and emotional angst are also charged with commonalities of finding community, finding solace in others, and ultimately finding themselves. This does not always lead to positive panaceas, but it does help to draw back the heavy curtains of depression when you know you are not alone.

The editors of this book, *Challenging Genders*, have presented an outstanding educational and emotional work that will help to dissolve the lines that separate us as well as lift the curtain of ignorance that permeates this subject.

Ms. Kari Samantha McAllister
Gender Lecturer
Library Commissioner, Hayward, CA
City of Hayward Anti-Discrimination Task Force, 2017–2018

Table of Contents

Introduction

This book has been a long time in coming. Non-binary people have been marginalized far too long in gender theory and existing literature, not to mention in all social institutions. From a lack of adequate research to a dearth of publications that highlight this distinctive group of people around the globe who, by their very nature and through living authentically, defy gender expectations and challenge people's belief systems, it is time their voices are heard.

These are people who challenge the gender dichotomy of strictly male and strictly female, which is a binary concept. These people are non-binary, and with that term of identity comes a variety of genders, even no gender at all.

With cultures all over the world who recognize there are so much more than two rigid, binary genders, it is time the Western world catch up to make room for people who have always been here. These are people who you meet and speak with every day. When you go to work, when you play your weekend sports, when you're grocery shopping – they are there. They are your doctors, your teachers, your hairdressers, your attorneys, your neighbors, your friends, and yes, even your children, siblings, and parents.

This book is an introduction into the lives of non-binary individuals; in this case, ones who were assigned female at birth (AFAB) by a doctor or midwife due to nothing more than that person looking at their genitals and declaring "It's a girl!" These are people who were perceived as and treated as female for a number of years before they took charge of their identities and said "No more! That's not who I am!"

Part I of the book is by no means comprehensive. The topic deserves so much more than what this book offers in terms of education. However, put together with Part II of the book, a compilation of stories by sixteen non-binary individuals, our readers will gain a deeper understanding of what it means to live as a non-binary person.

It is time their voices are heard, and who better to tell the story of non-binary lives than non-binary people themselves?

PART I

CHALLENGING GENDERS

1: Gender Identity

Science has shown evidence of more than just male or female sexes. Social science has also shown evidence there is more than two genders. For those who argue, it is because, many times, it is due to the conflation of the terms *gender* and *sex*. But what do we mean when we talk about *gender* and *sex*? How are they different?

We can look at what the academics and social scientists have told us over the years. John Money (1955) said that gender and sex were separate, and Nicolson (1994) pointed out that gender is causally constructed. Stoller (1968) explained the difference by claiming 'sex' is about biological traits, and 'gender' is the amount of femininity and masculinity a person exhibits. Butler (1980) then stated that gender was only true and real to the extent it is performed. Mikkola (2012, 2015) continues with Butler's train of thought three decades later, suggesting that if there were no heterosexism compelling people to engage in gendering acts, there wouldn't be any gender, and continued later, with stating that gender is socially produced, and as such, is changeable. Mikkola (2012) goes on to say that sex is unalterable or unchangeable, but individuals have control over gender because it can be altered and changed.

Devor (1989) suggested that the belief that sex determines gender is so commonly conflated that people use the terms interchangeably. Some people choose to believe that biological sex and gender are one and the same, even to the extent of believing their bodies are a reflection of their gender regardless of physical attributes. However, this idea is less popular than that of what sociologists, social scientists, medical scientists and gender scholars have recognized through recent years. Gender encompasses culture, social cues, and society standards – and is not confined to binary masculine or feminine, but rather spans the spectrum, and even, believed by some, to be outside the confines of a spectrum. The most complete description of gender that we have come across was written by Bornstein and Bergman in 2010:

> Instead of saying that all gender is this or all gender is that, let's recognize that the word gender has scores of meaning built into it. It's an amalgamation of bodies, identities, and life experiences, subconscious urges, sensations, and behaviors, some of which develop organically, and others which are shaped by language and culture. Instead of saying that gender is any one single thing, let's start describing it as a holistic experience (p. 87).

Let's go back to biology for a moment. People are born with certain attributes and body parts. Some have a penis. Some have a vagina. Some develop breasts. Some grow facial and/or body hair. Society has determined that those with a penis, facial hair, and the lack of breasts are male, while those who grow breasts and are able to conceive a child are female. There is a serious lack of acknowledgment, however, when it comes to the common occurrence of a baby who is born with genitals that are

4

not so easily defined by looking at them, or those whose chromosomes are not the standard XX or XY, but no one knows it unless there is a reason later on in life to suspect there may be a reason for physical traits being different than what society thinks they ought to be. This is called being *intersex*, and it is recognized by the medical community that not all human beings are born strictly male or strictly female. In fact, Haynes (2001) has determined there is a variety of at least seventy variations of biological sex.

You will see and hear many trans and non-binary people use the terms AFAB and AMAB. These terms clearly describe society's imposed sex (or gender) on a child – one is either Assigned Female at Birth or Assigned Male at Birth. This determination is made by the initial physical inspection of genitals and declared whether male or female, (thus, in effect, 'assigned') one or the other.

With this in mind, why do we not hear of or see intersex individuals as commonly recognized members of a society? They exist, they are around us in our daily lives, but many have adapted into either the appearance of binary male or female and 'blend in' with those around them. Creighton (2001) answers this by telling us that clinicians choose the gender that allows for the best prognosis for reproductive and sexual function, and which gives the most "normal" looking genitalia. Notice he talks about gender – not sex. He claims that in choosing in this manner, it will "ensure a stable gender identity" (para. 7). If we can overlook his ignorance and conflation of gender and sex, we can look at the real issue – doctors decide by looking at genitals whether a child is male or female, and if it doesn't look like what they deem is normal, they "fix" it by surgically altering it — without the child's consent, and without even a thought that it might not need fixed! Why must we as a society decide there are two, and only two, sexes? Who made us gods? No one – let us repeat this – *no one* can determine one's gender identity except the individual who is claiming their own gender. Doctor's cannot determine gender, they can only play god and announce (or create) a one-of-two-sexes being. What happens to that child in the future in terms of gender has nothing to do with the doctor — except when that doctor made the wrong choice in surgically altering the genitalia of that child. That individual, as an adult, now has a choice to make –live authentically in the gender they are, or live as the assigned sex they were given.

There are also those whose brains develop differently than what their physical body suggests, and this is recognized by both medical and social scientists as transgender individuals, and more recently being highlighted in media though they have existed for centuries, non-binary individuals. Stryker (2008) defined "transgender" as "the movement across a socially imposed boundary away from an unchosen starting place – rather than any particular destination or mode of transition." This term has broadened considerably since its inception in the 1960s, now encompassing individuals who have or desire medical treatments such as gender affirming surgeries and/or hormones to present or express themselves more masculine or feminine, as well as those who wish to appear more androgynous. Some people under this wide "umbrella" of transgender consider themselves "transsexual", while some consider themselves "trans", which has become the more common term for the wider community.

Still others feel they are neither male nor female, but rather somewhere either in-between or even outside of this spectrum. These individuals generally consider themselves non-binary. Some may call themselves trans, but others may not. There is no standard, no right or wrong, no rules or mandates that specify one must be trans to be non-binary. Nor are there any rubrics for trans people who consider themselves to be masculine or feminine, yet non-binary as well.

Society has given us two, and only two, sets of gender rules, and those who live outside of those rules are *challenging genders*.

2: Non-Binary Identities

From the moment we take our first breath...the cry 'It's a boy' or 'It's a girl' ushers us into this world. The genders we're assigned at birth lock us on to a course through which we'll be expected to become whole, well rounded, creative, loving people – *but only as men or as women* (Bornstein, 1998, p. 1).

All over the world in many cultures you'll find gender non-conforming people – those who are traditionally third gender or gender-fluid or even agender. In some of these cultures, they are not only recognized, but also revered and honored, or treated as spiritual beings. In Hawaii, one can find the *mahu*, those who are biologically male or female, but having a gender identity between or encompassing both masculine and feminine, and whose social role is sacred. Some Native American people are *two-spirit*, while South Asia has their third gender called the *hijra*. Other cultures recognizing a third gender are Nigeria (*yan daudu*) , Samoa (*fa'afafine*), Thailand (*kathoey*), Mexico (*muxe*), and Tonga (*fakaleiti*). In yet other cultures, it is socially acceptable that some third genders are those who were assigned male, but live and behave as feminine and those who were born assigned female but live and behave as masculine.

In all cultures there is evidence of a gender continuum, with effeminate boys and men and masculine girls and women. For some of these individuals, they acknowledge and celebrate their gender identity as something other than male/man or female/woman, while others simply live authentically without a thought of identity or gender.

The term *gender identity* means the individual's sense of being is either male, female or somewhere between or outside of these binary end posts. Some people are born assigned female at birth, but their gender identity is masculine, or even binary male, while others are born assigned male, but their gender identity is feminine, or even binary female. Many non-binary people lean towards one or the other, but few reach the "binary" status. Some don't feel they belong on either side – neither masculine nor feminine – but something entirely outside of these boundaries. They have a gender identity that is beyond that which society has deemed "normal" or "typical". For some individuals, there is no "opposite sex". For them, there is only identity.

Everything we do, and every interaction we have in life is based on gender – but only on male and female. Any identity outside of these binaries are unrecognized by the majority of society. In being classified as either male or female, one is expected to follow the rules – the typical gender roles associated with them. The rules tell us how to walk, talk, behave, and relate to others of both the "same" gender and the "opposite" gender. But the rules fall short when it comes to non-binary individuals. The rules don't always apply, and if they do to some extent, they may not in other areas.

As a for instance, girls/women or those perceived as such are socially accepted when wearing trousers and a button up shirt, even a tie and a casual jacket. People may see these individuals as masculine women, or just contemporary women or even label them a feminist– but they are generally accepted, nonetheless. However, when a boy/man or those perceived as such chooses to wear a dress, or perhaps a feminine blouse, or have colorful painted nails, they are quickly perceived to be gay (at best), or deviant, or a pervert. They are teased unmercifully, they become an outcast with their peers, unacceptable for employment, and all-too-often attacked verbally and even physically for their appearance.

For those assigned female at birth and have a gender identity other than girl or woman or female, the appearance is not necessarily the issue in their daily, casual life. It is likely an issue, however, when they are growing up and being told to look more feminine, or as adults when they are working in a job that requires a dress code which separates the genders into male and female apparel, Not only are they then forced to either comply with society's rules, or be punished for living authentically in their true gender, they are also subjected to the constant, daily misgendering as people perceive them to be female as well as they must endure the misogyny and sexism that comes with the perception of being a non-male individual.

Never, ever, mistake a person's personal gender identity on exterior appearance or behavior, because once again, there are no rules when it comes to non-binary individuals.

Research now suggests that children as young as two begin showing gender-related preferences, with boys engaging in masculine activities and girls engaging in feminine activities (Lee & Troop-Gordon, 2011; Lobue & DeLoache, 2011). As young as three or four years old, they perceive the differences of male and female, even genital differences in themselves and others, and they reach peak rigidity in gender roles by 5 or 6 (Martin, Ruble, & Szkrybalo, 2002). As young as five years old, they are implicitly and explicitly aware of their gender identity when it is not that of their assigned sex (Olson, Key, & Eaton, 2015). It has been shown that being out to parents as a transgender or gender variant youth results in higher frequencies of micro-aggressions, family-level child maltreatment and religiosity (Gartner & Sterzing, 2018).

In other words, gender non-conforming kids are targets of abuse from family members, and exposure to childhood physical, psychological, and sexual abuse is high compared to those without gender non-conformity (Roberts, Rosario, Corliss, Koenen & Austin, 2012). These gender non-conforming kids often experience ostracism from their peers, and when pressured to conform to gender norms, they become anxious, sad, and begin social withdrawal, self-deprecation and display other signs of distress (Cohen-Kettenis, Owen, Kaijser, Bradley, & Zucker, 2003; Carver, Yunger, & Perry, 2003).

Violations of gender norms are often met with peer rebuke and social sanctions, and for the greater majority of children, provoke greater gender-role conformity (Lee & Troop-Gordon, 2011). However, when the child is gender non-conforming due to a gender identity mismatch with their body, gender-role conformity doesn't come easily nor without causing deep distress to the child.

There are countless identities that can be considered as non-binary, and there are as many variations of expressing these identities as there are experiences of those who identify as something other than binary male or binary female. There are multiple terminologies people have adopted to describe their identities, including gender-queer, gender fluid, asexual, demigender, androgynous, enby, genderflux, neutrois, polygender, and many, many more. We found in our research for this book several other personal gender identities such as the following (and not limited to):

- mutligender
- bulldagger, third gender
- F.a.a.b. queer two-spirit (F.a.a.b. = Female assigned at birth)
- Neutrois
- agenderflux
- stonebutch
- Prettyboy
- Feminine boy, jeune garçon, fleur instead of soeur
- gender diverse
- boy thing

This book will not go deeply into all the definitions of all non-binary identities, but in sharing the stories by these sixteen individuals who have contributed to the book, our readers will be able to gain a clearer understanding of the experiences of many non-binary individuals.

It is very important in one's quest for understanding non-binary individuals and all that it encompasses to keep an open mind. When someone you know or encounter identifies themselves as a non-binary individual (with any one or more of the number of terminologies previously mentioned or even a different one altogether), you simply need to accept this as factual, use their requested pronouns, don't misgender them, and don't ask questions. They will tell you what they want you to know.

Understand, also, that not all non-binary people are necessarily transgender, so put that assumption aside. Some consider themselves cisgender, yet not a binary man/male or woman/female. As well, sexual orientations are all over the map with non-binary individuals. Some AFAB non-binary people might identify as trans feminine and lesbian, while others might identify as transmasculine and gay, and others might be bisexual, or pansexual, or asexual, or any other orientations and identities. Their sexual orientation is none of your business unless they choose to tell you.

Sexual orientation and sexual identities and labels are also not of concern in this book unless specifically addressed by one of the Contributors. Understand, too, that the term 'butch' and its variations are not strictly *lesbian* terms. Gay men and others have also been known to use this terminology, so it is not limited to AFAB individuals. Non-binary people consist of a plethora of sexual orientations, terms, and labels, none of which changes the fact that their gender falls into the category of non-binary, and in this book we are focused on *gender identities*.

'Butch' and its variations, in the context of this book as well as to many AFAB individuals all over the world, is a gender identity. It can be an identity in, or completely outside of, the Butch/Femme culture. It is generally (but not always) a more masculine or androgynous presenting (in appearance) gender identity. Those who consider themselves butch may or may not be lesbian, may or may not consider themselves under the trans umbrella, may identify as more feminine or more masculine, and most importantly, only they can make the distinction and decision they are, or are not, trans.

Some AFAB individuals who identify as butch use he/him/his pronouns, while others use she/hers, others use hy/hys/hym, and so on. Countless AFAB individuals who identify as butch encounter many of the same barriers, discrimination, and even violence that transgender people encounter in society. Research has shown that being butch is experienced as an "unmalleable aspect of self, so essential that it even preceded their awareness of that label" (Levitt & Hiestand, 2004). It is something that is deep inside, so deep one may not even have a word for it, but the knowledge of *being* is just that – it just *is*. Many describe themselves in childhood as tomboys, and socialized as boys rather than as girls, and even as adults are uncomfortable with feminine clothing or even being perceived as feminine (Levitt & Hiestand, 2004). This is, no doubt, a clear example and definition of what it is to be non-binary (or transgender). Those who are not masculine-appearing can also be non-binary in identity, despite a more feminine appearance.

Again, we cannot stress it enough. There are no "rules" or standards for being or identifying non-binary. Some are decidedly set in their appearance, mannerisms and vocabulary, while others are more fluid (genderfluid being just one of the fluid identities). There are also the matters of geographical location, religious or conservative upbringings, familial and peer pressure, environment and more that can, and does, affect the presentation of non-binary individuals. One need not "look" non-binary to identify as non-binary. *There is no one particular look or appearance for non-binary individuals.*

Behind the eyes of every Butch, Stud, Masculine of Center individual there is someone who 'comes out' every single time they step outside into the world, where being who they are is to risk facing intolerance daily. You cannot hide the swagger, the energy does not lie beneath. It might be accompanied by a buzz cut, a ribbed tee or a wallet chain, but those things are not defining as aesthetics alone. It's the energy. It

exudes from across any room and it carries the message that there stands an individual who is proud to represent their gender identity...Even in the face of those who oppose their presence, there they are in all their masculine glory daring to walk their walk. Like warriors. Messengers of acceptance.

--Daywalker

Respondents to our questionnaire for this book ranged in ages at the time of the questionnaire from 13 to 69 years old, with a median age of 25. Seventy percent of respondents had at least some college, with 19 percent of those having a Master's degree or above, and 82.5 percent identified as White.

One of the questions we asked was "At what age did you begin to understand and identify as non-binary?" The answers ranged from several of them at three years old to all the way up to 56 years old. Almost half (44%) of them knew they were non-binary before they were 18.
Another question we asked was "What does 'non-binary in regards to gender *mean* to you personally, in your words?" The overwhelming majority of the answers were straightforward in saying that it is 1) an umbrella term, and 2) it is a gender that is not 100 percent male nor 100 percent female, but somewhere in-between or outside of this continuum.

A few answers stood out, including one by Varick Michael Honeycutt, a 23-year old nonbinary transman pursuing their doctorate in order to provide crucial research, who wrote;

To me, it is a descriptor that represents my political stance against the idea that gender and sex are fixed dichotomies. A political stance against labeling my interests, hobbies, and personality, as something related to and fixed by sex and gender. A political stance against a broken system that needs to be dismantled as arbitrary and a means to maintain hierarchies and justify oppression against certain individuals in pursuit of power/privilege.

Some people feel that it is outside the binary, and synonymous with the word 'agender', while others feel that being androgynous is non-binary. In fact, one said they were not genderqueer, or genderfluid, because their gender doesn't change. They are both, and although they lean towards masculine, they are not a transman, because they feel there is a feminine identity in that term.

Another feels like he is his 'own man'. He doesn't identify as cis, doesn't feel like cis, and doesn't want to be seen as a cis man. Yet another individual says non-binary is who they are. They are genderless, and present masculine or feminine at different times. While another person who identifies as agender/non-binary, they believe they exist beyond the binary of gender and don't attribute any of their gender expression or identity to either of those binaries. How they dress, conduct themselves, and their interests are not byproducts of masculinity or femininity. They are byproducts of them.

Among the other descriptors of non-binary that we have seen include; freedom, multitudes, human, infinite genders, undefined space between defined areas, limitless, and transcending boundaries. So as you can see, there is no simple definition of what non-binary means. In fact, some people even spell it without the hyphen (nonbi-nary) and others use the hyphen in their identity.

3: Pronouns

Oftentimes throughout our human existence when something challenges the current social construct in a society it is called out as radical, or even trendy, when in fact some of these challenges are simply a reintroduction of our original thoughts from a time long ago. We are going to apply that specifically to the evolution of pronouns and the return to the language used to define and address those who identify as non-binary.

It's 2018, and the movement within Western Civilization and abroad to convert current pronoun usage to a non-sexed language has come to fruition in many realms. In America we have seen changes put in motion within State Universities, the New York Subway, and California and Oregon have made room for non-binary and gender non-conforming individuals by introducing a new gender marker on State Identifications that validate and recognize non-binary individuals.

Since the colonization of the Western world began, it arrived with the movement to trim society down to just two genders based upon the genitalia one was born with, and because of this, there have been many gender identifications slowly erased. It wasn't a box that was created, it was a straight line not to be crossed – or one would be called out as deviant and suffer the consequences of being born differently. As mentioned in a previous chapter, those born in variations of intersex conditions were often surgically manipulated to conform to one or the other, a decision made by physicians and parents that were sure that humans had to be 'one or the other' because they were not of the knowledge that gender is of the brain and not the born genitalia.

Some may credit this movement to Second Wave Feminists (with the introduction of Ms. replacing the binary Miss or Mrs.), and some may credit the predictable history of language repeating itself by recycling and reinventing how words are used. Others may even credit the World Wide Web for its frenzy of platforms that introduce case after case of how ridiculous the notion of one's biological assignment of male/female dictating the usage of he/she him/her, as it generally points to a set of stereotypical behaviors that fall in line with patriarchal ideas of what masculine/feminine behaviors should look like and who gets to display them.

Masculinity does not belong exclusively to men as femininity does not belong exclusively to women. For those who were assigned female at birth, this movement is more than just a phase. They have become the voices of resistance asserting that being addressed as 'she' equates to 'less than' in society, industry and government. Many pronoun options are being reborn and others are being created in this movement.

Social media platforms are broadening their gender identity categories. Facebook has accommodated their users by adding custom gender options, and as of 2015 they went a step further by expanding this feature to include a free-form field for folks to add their own. There are over 70 genders as of 2018, which is a clear sign that there is an obvious need to follow this up by expanding the pronoun options as well, so Facebook followed through by adding the same free-form option for pronoun usage. A statement from Facebook found on their Diversity page states that if one does not identify with their list of pronouns, one has the option to add their own, which gives them the ability to express themselves in an authentic way ("Facebook Diversity", 2018). Mobile dating search app, Tinder, added 37 new gender identity options in 2016 (Clarke-Billings, 2016), and others are following their lead. Time Magazine featured a story highlighting the fact that it is time to acknowledge we are beyond the 'He' and 'She' binary gender system, and that young people now are far more accepting of the different identities they encounter (Steinmetz, 2017). Colleges and universities have been changing their paperwork, and some, like Harvard, are allowing students to choose their gender-neutral pronoun (Corinne, 2018).

Laws and statutes have begun to change across the continent. In New York City, we saw a major victory in the push for the rights of those who are non-binary near the end of 2017. The NYC Commission of Human Rights released a list of gender-neutral pronouns to all businesses and landlords requiring them to use the pronouns or be fined as much as $250,000 "for willful, hostile and repeated misuse of pronouns" (Perez, 2017). Oregon and California the Courts have made landmark rulings in favor of those applying for gender marker changes that have neither an 'M' (male) nor 'F' (female). While the State Identification agencies are still scrambling for the software to print the new Markers on one's State Identification(s) they have put the wheels in motion and soon there will be a third gender field available.

These steps are monumental to the evolution back to a place in society where various pronouns were once celebrated and honored. The list of gender neutral pronoun suggestions is long, and it continues to grow, so we will not list them all here. Some of them are socially constructed and are facing backlash from opponents of gender neutral pronouns, while others which are more commonly used have been around for hundreds of years and are beginning to settle back into the English language.

We will share just a small number of the growing list of gender neutral pronouns here.

❖ *They/them/theirs* – Today's most often used gender neutral pronouns, with a History that spans back many centuries. They took a stumble in the early 1800s with a crusade by grammarians to rid the use as a singular pronoun and revert back to 'he' as a gender neutral approach in literature. Using 'he' as a singular pronoun is problematic in the process of achieving visibility and equality among those assigned female at birth. 'They' is making a huge comeback and may be the resolve to the conundrum of how to include all people no matter how they identify and in platforms where gender should not matter.

❖ *Hy/hym/hys* – Found in literary works as far back as the 13th century, this pronoun is still alive and well within the online Butch-Femme Community. This is a Culture which has been around for at least a

Century but now has found a need to differentiate between those who identified as more masculine than feminine on message boards, forums and social media platforms. This applies to masculine identified folks who were assigned female at birth and not a neutral pronoun as it sounds out the same as 'he/him/his'.

❖ *Ze/Hir/sie/zir* – Commonly used in the online genderqueer community, Ze is a modification of Sie (German for she) in order to veer away from the feminine sound. Hir (sounds like here) is a feminine pronoun from Middle English as well as a host of other languages. When read aloud within the English language, some people claim this set of pronouns runs into difficulty as a poser to neutrality due to the audible similarity to he/her as well as being awkward in its use when colliding with words that may begin and end with similar sounds that further feminize the subject of reference. Others find no fault with them and use them proudly.

❖ *Xe/xem/xyr/xyrs/xemself* – Steering from sie/hir in order to qualify as a neutral option. With the same pronunciation as Ze, some people feel that it, too, is awkward in its use when colliding with words that may begin and end with similar sounds.

❖ *Ne/nem/nir/nirs/nemself* – the attempt to move away from male or female reference patterns and differentiate itself by avoiding the letter H or S in front and opting for N which could be read to be intentional to pertain to Neutral.

- ❖ *Spivak (ey/em/eir/eirs/eirself)* – This is an interesting series that derives from 'They' but lost steam with a lack of use and quick interpretation, as it deviates too far from the original form and of course when spoken aloud 'em' sounds more like 'him' than 'them'.

- ❖ *Thon/Thon's/Thonself* - Created as a neoterism proposed by Charles Crozat Converse as a genderless pronoun meaning 'that one" or 'it'. Thon was removed from the Merriam-Webster dictionary for lack of use in 1961 but rode success long enough to be used in early 20th century crossword puzzles (Merriam-Webster, 2018).

- ❖ *Other pronouns* –We have found many others in our research include: tey/tem/ter/temself, e/em/eir/ emself, fae/faer/faers/faerself, and zhe/zhir/zhirs /zhirself, as well as several others not listed here.

Non-binary and gender neutral pronouns are more important to social evolution than at first it may appear. It's not just political, it's personal. It doesn't just matter to those who prefer them for themselves, but to those who do not as well. It is the English language (as well as others) in grammatical and literary circles that has failed time and time again to produce a neutral pronoun while many other languages have had them in place for centuries.

There are many languages which are grammatically gendered. In other words, nearly all nouns are dependent on grammatically using masculine or feminine correctly. French, Italian, Spanish, Hebrew, Hindi, and Portuguese are only a few of these languages. There are other languages that are grammatically genderless, such as Chinese, Finish, Hungarian, Vietnamese, and Turkish, for example. Some languages have included more than two grammatical genders, such as Polish, Czech and Slovak. English, although there are specific genders, nouns are not specifically gendered, and it is considered a *natural gender* language.

An interesting side note, research has shown that grammatically gendered languages are linked to higher levels of sexism. Out of 34 countries included in the World Economic Forum's Global Gender Gap Index, 54.5 percent predominately speak a gendered language, 19.4 percent speak genderless languages and 9 percent speak natural gender language (**Prewitt-Freilino, Caswe ll, & Laakso,** 2012). Here's the scoop, and it's not surprising. *Countries where gendered languages were predominant ranked lowest on the scale of gender equality.*

It's not hard to correlate why there is such slow progress of acceptance for neutrality of gender in the Western world when the history of academics with which folks are using to base their education lacks a history of examples for how to address one who is non-binary. It is up to this generation to be the educators and (re) create the history by emphasis and validation via every avenue at our disposal in the modern world; written and verbal until pronominal neutrals return to a state of normalized in languages around the world.

There is another facet of pronouns we will address in a later chapter, that of misgendering. Misgendering is referring to someone with a pronoun that is not reflective of the gender with which they identify. More on this later!

4: Gender Expectations

Gender stereotypes run rampant throughout all societies. Expectations of men and women, and the qualities ascribed to them are socially "required" and deviations of these expectations results in "punishment" and devaluation. Many products are gender-specific, and stereotyped (i.e. dolls for girls, action figures for boys), and the division of pink and blue clothing, or the ultra-feminine clothing for girls with the casual, relaxed look for boys. Advertising is targeted to gender-specific demographics, as are stories and television programs.

Early research which still holds validity today shows that there are separate components of gender stereotypes, such as traits, role behaviors, occupations and physical appearance, and each as a masculine and feminine version (Deaux & Lews, 1984). What is interesting is what these researchers found is when a person is given information about just one of these components, they use that information to infer other gender-related characteristics that are consistent with it. In other words, if given specific information about role behaviors, they make assumptions, or as the researchers put it, "they shape their estimates" (p. 998) of traits accordingly.

How many times has someone said they went to the doctor, and you automatically assumed the doctor was a man? Or your friend spoke of the great service from a flight attendant on a recent flight, and your initial assumption was the attendant was a woman? Think about a masculine presenting woman being assumed she is a lesbian simply because of her appearance. These are all classic examples of inferring gender-related characteristics from preconceived ideas about gender, roles, and behaviors.

Expectations due to stereotyping reflect existing differences in masculine and feminine, as well as they impact how people define themselves and are treated by others (Ellemers, 2018). There are differences between masculine and feminine, this is a fact. This researcher asks important questions – to what extent do these differences reflect who a person is, and to what extent does this result in how we should think about them because of stereotypes? Upon seeing a person, our perception of their gender is a primary feature in our thoughts or behaviors towards that person. When those thoughts and behaviors are prompted by stereotypes, the recipient doesn't always get a fair shake.

Stereotypes implicitly influence our expectations we have about "the qualities, priorities, and needs" of individual men and women (Ellemers, 2018) – this becomes a nightmare scenario for non-binary individuals who do not identify as a man or a woman. Most people don't want to admit they rely on stereotypes or have any gender bias, but the evidence tells us that stereotypes can be automatically activated and influence our behavior (Skorinko, 2018).

Expectations from every direction are thrown at non-binary people, from which bathroom they should use to what pronouns are to be used for addressing them. And speaking of bathrooms, think of the nearly impossible decision when an androgynous appearing person needs to use one. Do they use the women's and risk being yelled at? Or the men's, and risk being verbally, and possibly physically, attacked?

Ellemers (2018) appropriately states "Individuals who clearly violate stereotypical expectations capture our attention, and stereotype-inconsistent information can dominate our judgment", so we favor information that confirms a stereotype. An example of this, says this researcher, was shown in a study where participants received equal amounts of information on achievements and fame of both men and women, yet when they were asked to assess these unknown men and women, they relied on general stereotypical information to assign more fame to the men than to the women.

Research has shown that gender role socialization begins in infancy due to parental behaviors (Karraker, Vogel & Lake, 1995). Parents were observed over a 4-year time span and it was shown that implicit gender-role stereotypes and behavior increased over that time (Endendijk, Derks, & Mesman, 2018). These same researchers also showed that gender role stereotypes were more traditional in parents than non-parents.

But gender stereotyping isn't limited to just parents. It starts the moment the sex of the baby is declared in the delivery room. In fact, eighty percent of the first questions asked regarding a newborn are about the baby's gender (Intons-Peterson & Reddel, 1984). People treat their kids differently when they are growing up. Think about it... fathers spend time playing ball with their sons, while mothers have their daughters learning things in and around the home. Sons are often allowed out later in the evenings or to date at an age earlier than daughters. Sons are encouraged to play contact sports, while daughter are encouraged to pursue gymnastics, or tennis, or other non-contact sport. These 'encouragements' add up over time, and each time piles on one more layer of gender stereotyping.

West and Zimmerman (1987) claimed that doing gender isn't always living up to normative conceptions of masculinity and femininity, but rather it is engaging in behavior *at the risk of gender assessment*, and *this is the key take-away here*.

In most cultures, there are narrow definitions of masculinity and femininity, and when a person doesn't conform to the norms, they are bullied, harassed, and even physically attacked. Non-binary individuals, as we indicated in a previous chapter, often suffer consequences for their identities and non-conformance to societal norms.

5: Discrimination

Transgender and non-binary people find themselves oppressed, marginalized, and victimized in all social institutions. Their access to competent health care is hindered due to discrimination and reluctance of medical providers to work with gender non-conforming patients, and many educational settings are not prepared to protect the rights of transgender individuals. Few legal protections exist, although a few jurisdictions in the U.S. and other countries are slowly adding gender identity to their anti-discrimination policies and laws.

In the results of the first of two large-scale surveys of transgender community, many people are not aware that non-binary people were included. Many non-binary people consider themselves as trans or transgender, and may choose not to disclose their non-binary status. It is important to note, out of the 6,450 respondents to that survey, 860 (13 percent) of them chose to write in their gender in the Gender Not Listed box, and the majority of them wrote genderqueer or similar, such as pangender, third gender, Two-Spirit, and other non-binary terms (Harrison, Grant & Herman, 2012).

Here are just a few of the numbers found in a later, and much larger study (28,000 adults who identify as transgender in the United States) showing just how serious a problem discrimination is within the transgender and non-binary population.

- 29 percent live in poverty, compared to 14 percent in the U.S. population.
- 15 percent unemployment rate, compared to 5 percent of U.S. population.
- 77 percent of gender non-conforming youth in Grades K-12 have been harassed, mistreated, or assaulted (James, et al., 2016, p. 9).

Canada (Veale et al., 2015) shows similar statistics:

- 70 percent of trans or gender non-conforming youth report being sexually harassed
- 36 percent reporting being physically threatened or injured
- 65 percent of youth have seriously considered suicide, with more than a third attempting suicide at least once.

Specific to non-binary persons from the Transgender Law Center (Meerkamper, 2014):

- 19 percent reported job loss
- 90 percent reported anti-transgender bias on the job
- 78 percent who transitioned at the workplace experienced more discrimination.

Non-binary persons face discrimination in health care, too, and in the UK (UK Trans Info, 2015) we found that:

- 46 percent present themselves as binary to receive medical treatment
- 72 percent did so while using services.

- 20 percent self-medicate as an alternative to seeking health care, and 65 percent chose not to answer about this.

What are the reasons for these numbers? Why is discrimination against gender non-conforming people so high? It could be that labels, names or derogatory behaviors can act as self-fulfilling prophecies that justify prejudice and discrimination against a marginalized population. By enacting social roles, maintaining patterns of interpersonal interaction and receiving feedback from like-minded individuals, people can build and maintain their own identities; "One way we do this is by enhancing those aspects of our body and personality that conform to the common image of our gender and suppressing those parts of ourselves that don't fit. (Cohen, 2015, p. 166-167).

When a gender non-conforming person becomes visible, ideas of gender are challenged and it is comfortable and easy to view this behavior as a deviance from the norm. When someone is crossing or defying gender boundaries, some people are unable to relate and it is uncomfortable for them. Some react out of fear, others out of hatred of what is "different". These emotions and reactions are in direct correlation to their personally interpreted meanings of who and/or what a non-binary or transgender person might be. When these meanings are interpreted as negative, prejudice oftentimes leads to the discriminatory behaviors.

Verbal harassment at school and in previous work-
places has been hellish, to say the least. I'm now self-
employed to protect against that, since I can't get a job
at school or most stores/offices/etc as who I actually
am. I'm a freelance artist and programmer and hiding
behind a screen is really the only way I've found to
make money while not being discriminated against
(16, masculine-leaning genderfluid and trans,
they/them).

Gendered oppression, the systemic manner in which certain groups are privileged or disadvantaged because of their gender, is prevalent in what is considered to be a male-dominated, hegemonic society, and when a person appears to oppressors that they are "defying their natural gender", bias begins to form and discriminatory behavior manifests in the form of verbal harassment, physical abuse, and hate crimes toward gender non-conforming individuals.

The reality of discrimination is a social production, the meanings of which stem from the behavior other persons direct towards the object of discrimination. The behaviors come from their perceptions, and are the result of any number of factors, such as religious beliefs, familial trends, peer pressure, and previous interactions. Research has shown how some cisgender individuals describe trans or gender non-conforming individuals with terms such as "odd," "weird," "different," and "gross" (Gazzola & Morrison, 2014). Many, if not most of those who are gender non-conforming, whether non-binary or trans, have heard these terms and ones that are much,

much worse. It is society's way of punishing those who don't conform to the 'norms'.

> Rules for gender are associated with privileges and punishments as part of a system that privileges certain groups of people and oppresses others....privilege exists when one group has something of value that is denied to others simply because of the groups they belong to, rather than because of anything they've done or failed to do (Rands, 2009, p. 422).

These rules imposed by society "are constantly reinforced through the threat of ridicule, humiliation, and physical violence should an individual fail to abide by them" (Schifter & Madrigal, 2000, p.95). As you read previously, the high numbers of discrimination are both frightening and distressing.

Along with a male-dominated society, we can look at a large instigator of oppression and discrimination – sexism. Mentioned briefly in an earlier chapter, sexism is based on gender bias, stereotypes, and assumptions (Wilchins, 2004). These stereotypes are based on socially constructed categories that are accepted as 'normal' –a binary gender system – and the reactions toward those who display anything different than 'normal' is oppressive. These reactions happen not only to non-binary people, but people in societies everywhere – a man with 'man boobs' or a woman with some excess facial or body hair, for example, become targets for sneers and jokes.

Just to be clear, sexism isn't limited to just men's attitudes about women. Women do reject hostile sexism, but they often endorse benevolent sexism – rewarding women for conforming to the patriarchal status quo, which inhibits gender equality (Glick & Fiske, 2001). This, in turn, affects minority groups, which include transgender and non-binary people.

No one is exempt from the expectation of 'normalcy' when it comes to gender and appearance expectations. Nor is anyone immune when they challenge the stereotypical gender norms. How many times have we heard a woman CEO called a 'bitch' or an 'ice queen' when she displays the exact same attitude of assertiveness as her male counterparts, (who, in turn, are praised for their leadership abilities)? Men who are 'softer' in nature, opposite the 'he-man' appearance or attitude, are often accused of being gay, and bullied with accusations of 'faggot' and 'sissy'. Women who choose to wear their hair short, dress comfortably in slacks and a T-shirt, and raise their kids on their own are often called lesbians or 'dykes'. Homophobia and transphobia stem from disgust, fear and hatred, and, like sexism, occur because of the ingrained, implicit social expectations of a binary gender system.

Julia Serano (2007) argues that in Western culture, there are two main roots of sexism. The first is the prevailing belief that maleness and masculinity are superior to femaleness and femininity, and the second, which is crucial in the context of non-binary identities and which Serano calls *oppositional* is the equally prevailing belief that female and male are rigid, mutually exclusive categories. In other words, forced conformity to the binary. This mistreatment of women and non-binary people creates an imbalance of power and renders feminine and non-binary people as disadvantaged in society.

Sexism, with society's implicit beliefs in the power dynamics of masculinity and femininity, is just one of many instigators of discrimination of gender non-conforming people, and just one of the reasons gender nonconforming people experience high rates of physical and sexual assault, and police harassment, and also experience a significantly high rate of suicide attempts at 43 percent (Harrison, Grant & Herman, 2012). Compare this to the 0.6 percent of adults in the U.S. 18 or older who have made a suicide attempt (Shepard, et al., 2016).

Another serious problem for non-binary people that occurs on a regular basis is the discrimination from people within the trans or transgender community. Some binary trans people, possibly due to their own sense of gender identity being 'opposite' the assigned sex and their own indoctrination into the societal notion of only two genders, spend an inordinate amount of time finding ways of invalidating non-binary people. We have seen this over and over in certain social media groups where the topic of who is and who isn't really trans comes up on a daily basis. Non-binary people are automatically placed into a lower status by some transgender individuals, one that is even accused of being 'trendy' or 'fake'.

You may be asking why this happens. Some people seem to believe that one must have gender dysphoria to be transgender. What they are overlooking is that transgender is not just an identity, it's an umbrella term that covers all gender non-conforming people. This includes transsexual persons. In the past few months, some trans people have alleged that transsexual is an 'outdated' term (it is not, however), and they don't recognize that transsexual means a person desires to or has had medical intervention to change their outward appearance to more closely match their inner sense of gender identity. These same people overlook the fact that the prefix 'trans' covers both transgender and transsexual, and transgender means an gender non-conforming person.

The American Psychological Association has made it clear in their statements that non-binary (gender diverse, non-conforming, and so on) people can be considered transgender, and at the same time, dysphoria is not a requirement for being transgender (Mizock, Mougianis, Meier, & Moundas, 2015).

The World Professional Association for Transgender Health has made it clear in its latest edition of the Standards of Care v. 7.0 that, first and foremost, being transsexual, transgender, or gender nonconforming (note the three terms?) is a matter of diversity, and not one of pathology (Coleman, et al., 2012, p. 5). To explain this statement, they assert:

❖ Gender nonconformity refers to the extent to which a person's gender identity, role, or expression differs from the cultural norms prescribed for people of a particular sex;

❖ Gender dysphoria refers to discomfort or distress that is caused by a discrepancy, between a person's gender identity and that person's sex assigned at birth (and the associated gender role and/or primary and secondary sex characteristics), and;

❖ *Only some gender nonconforming people experience gender dysphoria at some point in their lives.*

We ask you, the reader, where do non-binary people turn when their own community disregards them and bullies them for being authentic? They are not only unsafe in society, but they are also unsafe in the marginalized community where they are supposed to belong.

This brings up another form of discrimination that we said earlier we believe deserves its own chapter – the topic of misgendering. As you can see by the numbers, it is a common occurrence. These numbers are only what these respondents have found as their *biggest obstacle*, but a considerably high number of non-binary individuals around the globe report misgendering is a regular and significant problem in their day-to-day lives.

When asked what the biggest obstacle they have encountered as a non-binary individual:

- ❖ 26 percent said being misgendered
- ❖ 13 percent said problems with public bathrooms
- ❖ 8 percent have experienced harassment or violence

The remaining obstacles included dismissal/ invalidation from the trans community, incorrect pronouns, loss of family/friends, loss of employment, inability to find a suitable identity label, and 'other'.

6: Misgendering

Misgendering – one of the most often used intentional forms of harassment, discrimination, and bullying.

Misgendering means using a word – typically a pronoun – that doesn't correctly reflect the gender with which a person identifies. Non-binary people use a variety of pronouns as you read in an earlier chapter, and being referred to as something other than one's gender is abusive and bullying. And it happens. Every day. To nearly every non-binary individual. Around the world.

To put it another way so it is very clear:

Intentional misgendering is discrimination.

To illustrate just how pervasive and common misgendering is, we did our research into previous literature. Keep in mind the results of the following study performed in 2017 were published in 2018, so they are very recent in relation to the publishing of this book. Although the survey used the word transgender, it included non-binary individuals in the way the five total questions were worded. Although they could have used one of the more common phrases, either "assigned male at birth" or "assigned female at birth", they used a word that resonated with the general population by saying "considered male" and "considered female". We find this acceptable, as in our own research, we have found that very few cisgender people know what 'assigned' gender is, and not all trans and non-binary people are using the terms at this time.

To find out global attitudes on trans and gender non-conforming people, a survey by researchers Clark, Boyon, & Jackson (2018) that spanned 27 countries and consisted of nearly 20,000 participants aged 18-64 asked the following question:

"What pronoun would you use when speaking about each of the following people who dress and live as one sex even though they were born another?"

There were two scenarios listed:

1. a person who was considered male at birth but dresses and lives as a woman, and;
2. a person who was considered female at birth but dresses and lives as a man.

There were four answers to choose from:
   a) A masculine pronoun (English: He/him)
   b) A feminine pronoun (English: She/her)
   c) A neutral / non-gendered pronoun (English: They/them), and;
   d) Don't know

Results showed that *people in the United States were the most likely to purposely misgender a transgender or gender non-conforming person.* Australia came in second with three out of five people who would do so. Two out of five people in the U.S., UK, Australia, and Canada were willing to use the appropriate pronouns 'he' for a transgender man and 'she' for a transgender woman.

Here's the kicker and the difference when it comes to misgendering non-binary people - *only one in five said they would use the gender-neutral pronoun 'they' to refer to a non-binary or gender non-conforming person.*

This is yet another example showing how non-binary individuals can and do experience high rates of discrimination comparable to transgender people. In fact, according to Harrison, Grant & Herman (2011), "gender variant respondents are suffering significant impacts of anti-transgender bias and in some cases are at higher risk for discrimination and violence than their transgender counterparts" (p. 23).

Research has shown that non-binary people report being misgendered more often than transgender men or women, and misgendering is shown to be psychologically disruptive and distressful (McLemore, 2015; McLemore, 2018). Misgendering is a subtle form of stigma that has the potential of influencing how a person feels and how they evaluate themselves and their social identity. When one's identity is not accurately verified by others, they experience negative affect, anxiety, and depression according to the researcher, and a significant amount of participants feel very stigmatized when they are misgendered (McLemore, 2018).

Misgendering can also be considered a microaggression. Sue (2010) tells us that microaggressions are everyday verbal, nonverbal, and environmental slights, snubs, or insults, and whether intentional or unintentional, they communicate hostile, derogatory, or negative messages to target persons based solely upon their marginalized group membership. These microaggressions might appear harmless or trivial, but they have a powerful impact on the psychological well-being of marginalized peoples, as evidenced in the previous research.

Microaggressions can include addressing a non-binary person with incorrect gender pronouns, but there is more. Calling someone by their former name, asking about their 'real' identity, failing to acknowledge their pronouns or name at all, or asking them to explain their gender are all forms of microaggression. Micro-aggressors can display 'gender entitlement', such as they have the ability to know the person's 'true' identity, and that their perception of the person is more valid than the person's own knowledge of their identity (Nordmarken, 2014).

Nordmarken (2014) goes on to give a fairly detailed description of microaggressors, including that they may communicate negative emotions and behaviors such as disgust, dismissal, confusion, shock, skepticism, agitation, and other discomforts when learning of a person's gender identity. They may become defensive if corrected or reminded, they might stare, avoid eye contact, laugh or look away, as well as make excuses or apologize excessively, which only serves to draw out the uncomfortableness. The researcher concludes this train of thought with "Regardless of intention, microaggressive behaviors often indicate that individuals perceive difference, communicating othering messages" (p. 131).

Yet another effect that microaggressions have on non-binary people is that they face the near-constant erasure when they are forced to misgender themselves on documents asking for their gender or sex, including birth certificates, passports, and driver's licenses (Robinson, 2014). Because of this erasure, they are many times ignored completely, or they are hindered as employees to engage or excel as a top employee.

Non-binary people face the absence of their gender in surveys, in sports which delineate between male and female sex, in public bathrooms when there are no gender-neutral bathrooms available, in support groups and meetings of all types which are specifically for women, or men, with no allowance for those who might be either or neither, and the list goes on. Day Walker expresses that feeling of erasure when they said "I'm still looking for the third option to appear. The box marked 'Other'. I still feel like I do not belong in the 'girls' line or the 'boys' line" (Day Walker, 2016).

A genderqueer blog writer, Sam Dylan Finch (2014), explains about misgendering someone. What it says to the person, among other harmful (and selfish) things, is

"I would rather hurt you repeatedly than change the way I speak about you."
And, of particular importance, you are also telling them,

"Your sense of safety is not important to me."

Misgendering someone might out them as non-binary or trans, it could risk their job, their housing, their friends, or even their life. Laverne Cox, a well-known transgender celebrity has stated her views on misgendering on multiple occasions. "Misgendering people is an act of violence.... Pronouns matter" (Choi, 2015).

Violence is not always physical. Violence can be psychological, and includes the exclusion of persons, the application of stigma, and efforts to deny human dignity. This often comes in the form of microaggression, which as we said previously, are hostile, derogatory, or negative messages aimed at a marginalized person – including by way of misgendering.

Many non-binary people cannot legally change their gender markers on their identity documents. Only a handful of jurisdictions in the U.S. and other countries allow any sort of non-binary designation, commonly an 'X' in place of 'M' or 'F', and for those who go by a binary pronoun that doesn't match their gender presentation, they are often exposed to abuse and discrimination, and they are faced with the constant burden of having to explain themselves to various public officials, insurance representatives, and others. This also means that in their jobs, applying for housing, loans, insurance, signing up for any type of social function, they are immediately put into a situation where they have to show a mismatched ID or succumb and 'pretend' they are the gender on the identification card. This puts them in the position of feeling shame, anger, sadness, and any other number of negative emotions they should not have to endure, simply because society won't dignify or acknowledge their right to live authentically.

Research has shown that people who are misgendered frequently feel that their identity is very important, but they experience lower self-esteem around their appearance, and have a reduced sense of strength and continuity in their identity (McLemore, 2015).

People say they respect me but then go on to misgender me because using my pronouns makes them uncomfortable (18, non-binary, they/them, Great Britain).

People must learn to show respect to all individuals, even if it makes them uncomfortable. To use only pronouns we are familiar with is to intentionally hurt those whom we claim we love. If they are friends, associates, co-workers –we expect a level of respect from them towards us, it is only natural that they expect that same level of respect. Their gender identity doesn't harm anyone. But your choice to ignore it or force the wrong one on them harms them.

7: Non-binary Voices

Our research for this book came from a variety of sources, including from an anonymous questionnaire over a several-month period. People from many countries gave us insight into many real life issues which non-binary people encounter. The participants were aware their responses could potentially be used in this book with the promise of full anonymity. The following are only a handful of responses, with the individuals identified by age, gender identity and pronouns, and occasionally by country of origin to show the diversity around the globe.

A 39-year old from the United States who came to terms with their gender identity of agender three years earlier shared:

I was born female, but identify as a half step between male and female and as such as neither of both genders....I do not identify as a woman, or a man, therefore he and she do not apply to me. I wish to be addressed as they, since I am between two genders and outside of the binary (sometimes followed by a discussion how they is not a singular pronoun blah.)

But growing up in a society that put transgender documentaries into the night programme and only talked about male to female transitions, was not helpful in finding a word to describe myself. I believe that non-

binary is still unknown in my home country. Even after realizing myself and researching what I felt, I still had a hard time to find the right label. I'm still not sure if agender is the correct word, but it's the closest match and that's okay, for now.

The biggest obstacle they have encountered is dismissal and invalidation from the trans community. They continue sharing their experience of the negativity that they encounter all too often.

People seem to have a problem to separate gender and sex. I was asked if my genitalia is a pineapple, if I'm a floating unicorn. Kids half my age felt the need to "learn me a thing or two" about gender biology. I was made fun of, called mentally sick, delusional, attention-whoring, a stain on the transgender community, a Satanist (no idea where that came from.) I was told that my identity is nothing but a new age thing in order to feel special, that it is impossible to be agender in a gendered society, that I'm a tumblerina, an attack helicopter, a 'disgusting fetishist'... etc. etc. etc. It has come to the point that I feel embarrassed explaining my identity to people, believing that they won't acknowledge me as I am anyway.

A 51-year old also from the U.S. who identifies as butch or genderqueer with he/him/his pronouns finds they are most comfortable in butch/femme spaces, and one of the biggest obstacles encountered is public bathrooms, and as he puts it

The uncomfortableness of people around me in public when they can't quite figure me out.... The majority of

my experiences have been subtle and tend to center around things like not getting service in restaurants, harassed in public restrooms, the looks/comments from strangers.... I present in a very masculine way. My hair is cut in a very short men's style. I wear only men's clothes. I don't bind, or even attempt to pass as male for the most part, though I often do without trying. Being able to present in the ways that I can tends to offset the things I can't change.

A 44-year old American who came to terms with their non-binary-ness twenty years earlier identifies as third gender, or Ergi, which is a Norse term, uses he/him/his as well as they/them/their pronouns. When asked about their identification under the trans umbrella, they shared,

I live across gender boundaries, at least the generally culture ones. I have medically transitioned so I fit that definition. I dress and do what feels right for me, some may interpret it as feminine, some as masculine. Often times different people in the same situation will interpret the same interpretation differently. English and our culture aren't good at describing things that don't fit into tiny boxes. Gender is definitely one of those things.

A 23-year old from Great Britain describes their identity as neurogender and neuroqueer, but uses the terms non-binary and genderfluid socially, and they use both she/her and they/them as pronouns. When asked how they explain pronouns to those around them, they answered:

I don't understand gender - it just seems like a weird personality trait that a lot of people mistakenly think develops at birth. Rather than labelling theory, and actual first conceptions of personal gender arising at best evidence around 3 years old. But anyway, I explain my pronouns as "use any pronouns for me except it. I'm not an 'it', but I am just a person whose gender is intangible anyway. I wish people would mix it up".

They go on to explain how their gender identity evolved into what it is...

I knew I wasn't a cis woman my whole life. But being pressured into presenting femme by everyone except my mother. [It] made me think for a while without having the words to express it as a preteen, I was a trans man. But now, I think I was just Not Cis and frustrated af with being told I must be. Then at uni, I didn't think about it until second year, when I really started reading a bunch of stuff, and settled on nonbinary. Genderfluid also matched my wavering preferences for identity and expression. They're also umbrella terms, so people shouldn't be able to argue with them as much (unfortunate though that this was a consideration). But in general I'm super vague because my understanding is super vague. Not like we had gender exploration classes in school, college, or uni at any point. Although growing up on absurdly binarist US military bases probably made me even more angry given the other intolerant crap they do.

A 27-year old non-binary, genderfluid individual in the U.S. has this to say when asked if they considered themselves trans:

54

I consider myself to be more on the trans end of the spectrum than cis. The problem is that I want to present myself as being more androgynous than I physically look, but I'm afraid to take hormones because I'm not completely unhappy with my appearance. I'm afraid I will feel worse about myself from the side effects. I would feel like I'm doing it for others instead of myself, to drive the point home, because I feel like I need to "prove" my gender identity.

Everyone sees me as a "lady" or "ma'am" and every time someone says that (which is multiple times a day, even from people I know), it feels like a knife in my heart. I tell myself that it's stupid to feel that way, but I know I shouldn't ever feel invalidated. I tell myself to accept the way I am... But I DO accept myself. It's other people that bother me. It makes me hate them.

I've been growing my hair out and I've been receiving a lot more of this. Even though I feel like I look better with long hair, it makes me feel like it's my fault for my dysphoria even more because I'm choosing a feminine feature. I wish I could do the things that I feel make me look good AND be seen as the person that I am within, and not experience dysphoria almost every second of every day that I'm outside my house. This is a really, really big problem for me.

A 45-year old identifying as two-spirit and using they/them/their pronouns has this to say when asked why they don't consider themselves as trans (or under the trans umbrella);

I've come to see myself as something in between male and female. Other than female body parts, I don't see myself as a female at all. However, I don't see myself as male either. I feel as if I'm something in between the two genders. Even using "trans" as an umbrella term, seems insufficient to describe how I view my gender.

On the biggest obstacles they have encountered, a 24-year old agender person in Norway says

"Feeling like I don't have a space in society; so both in mis-/gendering, the toilet problem, work titles; it feels as though I'm not welcome and don't belong."

A 19-year old queer person writes,

"Being nonbinary isn't some cute little choice I make to be a "special snowflake". I have finally found the words to describe how I have felt about my gender since I was a child. There is also no one or right way to be nonbinary."

When asked how they combat their dysphoria, a 25-year old transmasculine non-binary person who uses he/him and they/them pronouns shared the following:

I bind my chest, wear baggy clothes, stand and walk with my shoulders forward (in order to hide chest), talk in a deeper voice, get a haircut, buy something from the men's department, pack with a sock or packer, draw my eyebrows on darker, wear a rash guard vest when swimming, let everybody know I'm trans (as in a 'loud and proud' kind of way, because then at least they'll know my body isn't supposed to be like this). I also use the men's bathroom. I cry a lot and listen to a playlist I made of songs about trans experience or songs that remind me of that so I don't feel alone. I hang out with trans friends. I also use online forums such as TMSA UK to gain support, ask questions, and vent.

When asked what they would want people to know, a 17-year old who describes themselves as non-binary answered;

> *I just want people to understand that our identities are real, they exist, they are valid. that's the most important thing for me. I have equal amounts of fear and hope when I think of the future, and I deeply wish that my hopes come true and that my fears don't.*

An 18-year old in Slovenia who identifies as non-binary, uses they/them and she/her pronouns, and presents themselves as feminine has a tough time trying to explain their pronouns,

> *It's difficult because in my language we have genders for almost every single word and it's difficult to use something else. I just explain my identity and if we were to talk in English how they should use my pronouns.*

An 18-year old demi-girl in India has not yet come out due to her geographical location.

> *My country is conservative. Even if it becomes legal, I guess I'll still be harassed…. Here people don't understand things! So no question of coming out now…. non binary is often considered as only intersex or*

trans.. So people don't want to recognize us…. It's important that I accept myself. Everyone should do that. I was born a female but I identify as non binary demi girl... I have accepted myself and all I need is to make myself presentable.

Non-binary-ness comes in all forms, including those who are on the more masculine side of the gender continuum and in lesbian relationships. A 31-year old butch/masculine of center individual from Portugal says one of her biggest obstacles as a non-binary person is the inability to find a suitable identity label. She says,

I am more comfortable coming out as "lesbian" than I am with non-binary. Close friends know of my orientation but not how I identify. I wish to be recognised by merit before anything else. [She has experienced] *bullying at high school, mild violence, physical fights,* [and] *spat on. On occasion on the street harassment, name calling exclusively from males.*

When asked what she wants people to know or understand, her questioning of herself and society is apparent when she writes,

"No one is born a woman, we become one" (S. Beauvoir). This sentence has been a recurring thought when I think of my identity. If I were a child today and was given the opportunity I would take it with 100% certainty that I was in the wrong body. In puberty my dysphoria (breast) was through the roof. Today, however, I see myself more of a Masculine of Center woman than a man. I still do not fit the role society assigns to women yet today I would not consider myself fully a

man. However, I could do without my breast -though if no one pays them attention I'm fine. And I can't imagine wanting to become pregnant but would love to be able to "father" a child. So back to Beauvoir, I think I will never know if it was the fact that I was raised female and lived life from a woman's standpoint that makes me feel that I would be losing part of myself if I transitioned gaining to little in return. Maybe I ...am just not the "woman" society expects me to be.

A 21-year old agender demi-boy from South Africa tells about the discrimination and negative experiences he has encountered since coming out as non-binary at 19 years old,

My mother has psychologically abused me my whole life. She has bullied me at every turn, and when I came out to her she nearly killed me. She tried to force me into conversion therapy, and even sent me to a religious leader to be exorcised. When it turned out I couldn't be "cured", she told me that I was better off committing suicide. My stepfather has anger management problems and lashes out when he's annoyed. I've often been on the receiving end of his transphobia, homophobia, bigotry and racism, simply for trying to stand up for other people. Since coming out to them I've been cut-off financially, and have been living with friends until I can get back on my feet.

A 20-year old genderfluid, agender/male from Belgium is unable to come out except with his girlfriend. He writes,

I got severely bullied at school when I was in primary

school because I had said that I felt more like a boy than like a girl. People from my class started calling me "monster" and bullying me. Since I live in a small city, everybody knew that and as I grew up, people still called me monster and assumed I was a lesbian so I couldn't befriend with girls and boys would make fun of me because they said I "tried to act like a boy while I'll never be one".

I'm not out [now] because here people don't know about non binary and they would not understand. I sometimes say things like "I'm not a girl" or "Being a girl doesn't define who I am" but I never say "I'm non binary". I already tried explaining to some people but it is hard because they just don't understand... Since being in a relationship with my girlfriend makes me feel more confident and since she's one of the only person I came out to, I became more confident about my gender. I used to think I had to be masculine so that people won't misgender me. Now I accept more of my feminine side and I'm happy being androgynous.

Although there are several ways we could have chosen to end this first part of the book, a 20-year old non-binary Canadian shares something that we have agreed is the best ending before moving into the next part and reading the real life experiences of our sixteen contributors.

To all non-binary people...:

As long as you are comfortable in your own skin and your own identity, it doesn't matter what other people thing about you. Push past the people who disregard you, who misgender you, and who don't support you, and be the strong and magnificent human you are! I know that even though strangers don't necessarily know or understand that I am non-binary, it doesn't change who I am and it doesn't affect my life. Be strong.

PART II

OUR STORIES

Contributors

Aitijhya Kar is a teenager from Kolkata, India. She is a currently preparing for medical exam. She is an amateur writer, who also loves reading, photography, travelling and exploring. She is a feminist and is actively associated with the SAGA (Sexuality And Gender Alliance) community. She runs groups over social media which have become safe places for people to come out and seek support. She hopes to become a doctor and research more about the gender identities. She can be reached at parnassus2dovecotte@gmail.com and on Facebook @Tiara Aitijhya Periwinkle.

Alyssa Hillary is an Autistic, nonbinary PhD student in neuroscience at the university of Rhode Island and a mathematics instructor with the Art of Problem Solving. They are interested in issues of neuro-divergence, queerness, and representation. Their work has appeared in *Criptiques* and the *Spoon Knife Anthologies*.

Caden Rocker identifies as a Non-Binary/FTM/Trans*/Human, and is currently 34 years old. They grew up in Upstate New York and began to discover their true gender identity at the age of 22, after moving away from their hometown. Currently ze lives in Albuquerque, New Mexico where they have been an active member of the activist community for a few years. Caden has previously had work published before with a personal narrative published in *A Herstory of Transmasculine Identities. An Annotated Anthology*, by Michael Brown with other contributors. Rocker has also had various poems published as part of collections including a poem in *Our Voices. A collection of Poems on Abortion from New Mexicans*. In addition to writing, Caden enjoys is a passionate photographer, who also enjoys the outdoors, learning, music, and spending time with their dog, Cooper.

Emil Eichelberger, 26, is a clinical social worker who currently practices in the Piedmont-Triad area of North Carolina where they focus on providing trans and non-binary folks with inclusive and affirming clinical services. They have been heavily influenced by their own experiences with identity development having identified as genderqueer since they were 20. Their hobbies include writing, fitness, and cooking.

Gyps Curmi is a gender-diverse person of colour currently doing their PhD at Southern Cross University on the experiences of local people beginning their gender-transition in later-life. They have had several short stories published, including in peer reviewed journals, and won an international short story competition. Gyps has also begun a speculative fiction novel written entirely in gender-neutral language.

Jo Smiley is a writer from Louisville, Kentucky. They received a BA in English from Hanover College in 2014, and a MA in Journalism from the University of Missouri in 2017. Jo's passion is for storytelling, and they have been writing stories since they were in high school, and poetry since they were in elementary school. Their main goal with writing is to tell stories that are meaningful to people. They also have a few novels in the works that they are expecting to publish in the next few years.

64

Kai Yves Avery is an incalculable, childish, surrealistic dreamer of undefined gender living in a country currently in a state of flux and uncertain if it wants to progress or deteriorate. Writer of dark fantasy and science fiction, lover of coffee shops and worshipper of decaf. Married to a beautiful genderfluid individual since 2005, Kai is an inept homemaker, but a superb vegan cook.

Lis Regula is an assistant professor of biology, married to his life partner for 17 years. He lives in Kent, Ohio where he's (possibly too) involved in the community, with one of his children and spouse. His calendar is kept full with board meetings, gardening, fitness, mentoring youths, and generally causing trouble for the less progressive folks in town.

Maxfield Sparrow is a nomadic Autistic activist and writer, author of *No You Don't: Essays from an Unstrange Mind* and *The ABCs of Autism Acceptance*. He is currently working on a memoir about autism, emotions, and the first year of medical gender transition. Information about his writing and public speaking is at www.sparrowrose.com.

Morgan West is a 22 year old transgender man living in Kentucky. After earning his Associate in Applied Science, he spent two years living in New York City, where he was an active member of the local queer community, and worked at an adolescent health clinic serving many LGBT clients. His time as a part of this community brought a better understanding of himself and his fellow transgender individuals, along with a sense of inner peace knowing he was surrounded by acceptance and understanding. He has since moved back to his hometown, where he works as a military service representative for a federal health insurance contractor, and is grateful to serve his country in his small part. He remains an advocate his LGBT siblings by living as an openly gay, transgender man and being a positive influence in his community. He is highly family-oriented and enjoys spending his free time connecting with his parents, sisters, grandmother, and closest friends.

Moss Billman lives in a weird little room in a weird little house in a weird little city where it rains a lot. Sometimes they make tacos at night while swigging orange juice straight from the carton, in clear defiance of sanitation and a sense of human decency. They grew up in the Midwest, and are still trying not to apologize for that.

Sam Lacovara is a transmasculine twenty-something who works in the nonprofit sector coordinating a Sexual Assault Response Team in New York. They graduated with a Bachelor of Arts in Women's, Gender, and Sexuality Studies from SUNY New Paltz, where they participated in activism and organizing projects including New Paltz Feminist Collective, Take Back The Night, New York Students Rising, and others. Their interests include veganism, talking about Feelings, and queering marriage with their partner.

Sav grew up in a tiny coastal town just north of Perth, Western Australia. In their twenties they accumulated a couple of university degrees but decided not to put them to use. Instead, they spent a good few years exploring the world. They finally grew weary of life on the run and are now working toward a PhD in Gender Studies and enjoying the hustle and bustle of inner-city Melbourne.

Sé Sullivan, PhD is a white Genderfluid Queer activist scholar. Sé has been active in seeking the rights of marginalized individuals and communities for over 30 years in and out of academia. As a survivor of the psychiatric practice of reparative therapy as a child, Sé is dedicated to working towards the destruction of the Medical Industrial Complex as a means that creates pathologies for the policing of bodies. Another key area of focus is the dismantling of white supremacy as the methodology and structural underpinnings in which capitalism thrives and continues to reify difference globally to profit the few.

Shalen Lowell is an author, blogger, and poet from Boston, Massachusetts. As a trans and agender author, Shalen specializes in fiction which represents the intersection of fantasy and postmodern genres and queer literature. Shalen currently holds a B.A. in English Literature and Environmental Science. Their work is featured in Aether and Ichor, The Writing Disorder, and to be published this fall, in a forthcoming sociological text reader for college classes entitled Privilege through the Looking Glass.

Trystan Craigo is a part-time writer by hobby. While he has felt himself to be in many places on the queer spectrum throughout his life, he has only recently come out as transmasculine and begun his social transition. Trystan is an avid fan of all things nerdy, including sci-fi, fantasy, superheroes, games, fiction of all sorts, and playing with words and imagery. Music is also a huge part of his life, and he has recently found his niche in the

LGBT community with a men's choir in Colorado Springs, where he lives with his two partners and two cats.

Author: Aitijhya Kar
Age – 19
Non-binary Demi Girl

8: Discovering Me
2017

Prevalent gender norms indicate you're either a male or a female. What if you're different? What if you're not just male or female?

I was born a female, with a feminine body and a feminine self. From childhood, I've been taught to love my body, to love myself and surely I grew up to love my entire self, my femininity. Even the first sign of puberty was perceived with great glee, rather as bliss. My parents told me I've become a woman. But that's perhaps where my inclination towards femininity halted. I never experienced what other girls of my age did. I neither had an inclination towards make-up, pretty dresses, jewelry, nor did I have lots of teenage crushes. My hormones were pretty dormant. I felt that I lacked the typical enthusiasm most teens experience. I was shy and least interested in beautifying myself. My gender expression matched more to that of a pre pubertal female.

By virtue of my birth as a female, many constraints were implemented upon me. I was expected to behave in a feminine way. There have been ample instances where my assigned gender had become the judgmental factor for my capability, strength and tolerance. All through my pre-teen and early teenage, I felt like being surrounded by a cocoon of superficial femininity. I had to wear a mask of someone I couldn't really relate to. Predefined roles were like walls surrounding me. Disgust and depression had clouded my mind. All I wanted was to break free. That was the first time, the sturdy, broadshouldered teen gathered enough courage to stand in front of the mirror and say, "It's perhaps time to rethink who I am." Finally the superficial mask fell off. Finally the butterfly was ready to come out of the cocoon.

One day I told my best friend about how I feel. She shouted out, telling me I'm not normal and I should immediately consult a doctor.

I was indeed taken to a doctor, who said things will take a good turn with time. Things surely took a good turn, only to make me realise my true self, my non binary self. Social media was indeed a bliss and it opened to me the doors to the distant horizon. Gradually I came to know about the whole Spectra. I was literally thrilled to come across so many gender identities/expressions. I made new friends online who helped me to find out what label suits me (yeah, I love labels). My quest continued as I came across websites, where I used to read expert articles about the Non binary people, their psychology, their ways of identifying themselves. Expanding my friends circle added to my knowledge. Reading and talking to non-binary people removed even the faintest trace of psychological dysphoria that I used to experience. It was indeed a great achievement for me.

I live in a conservative country, India. It's not like there are lots of barriers curbing our freedom but indeed we're tied by the shackles of society. Whatever is uncommon or less is considered to be abnormal or unacceptable in the otherwise accepting country. Most people strongly disapprove of "non-masculine males" and "non-feminine females". Expressing my gender in public has really been a hurdle for me and I'm still struggling to win it.

For example, we have seats in public transport reserved for females; but I feel it's immoral to ask a gentleman to evacuate the seat just because he's not "female". I am strongly against such discrimination. I'm often criticized for not "grabbing" the opportunity to seat in a "Ladies'" seat. I've also faced incidents where a gentleman has offered me the "Ladies'" seat and I had declined it and restrained myself from the immoral act. The fellow passengers rebuked me saying, "You are a "Ladies ("yes, that's what they say), so you should sit there". Honestly, I still don't know how to make them understand I'm not a female, I don't feel a female, I'm just born a female. I really don't know how to even raise my point. So I tend to avoid situations where gender becomes decisive but not all situations are avoidable. While some might highlight this as a purely social issue, it appears to me as a boulder in the path of personal freedom of gender expression.

School had never really been a safe place for me. Growing up with cis and typical feminine girls was a constant source of insecurity. I've always felt that I do not belong. I've been a victim of bullying and verbal harassment quite a number of times. A few of my friends defended me but there was lack of strong support. Expressing my point of view resulted in more chaos and the best way was to ignore!

Coming out to friends have been relatively easy, yet not so easy. All of my friends, without a single exception had been unaware of the existence of non-binary individuals. Upon my enlightening them with the knowledge, I received diverse reactions. Some of my friends, very few though, were willing to accept me the way I was. My gender didn't matter to them, my friendship did. They were keen to discover the different facets of non-binary people with great glee. Another group of friends were not at all interested in my gender identity, they still continued to be friends as before, but my gender expression created a subtle hesitation on my part. Of course I couldn't discuss things with them. And the third group considered of the people with negative reactions. "You are what?", "But I can see you're a girl!", 'So you're neither a girl nor a boy, are you crazy?" – Such reactions were most common. Explanations didn't work, there was resentment all around. Most people felt I was in a phase or rather following a trend. Getting such reactions from close friends was indeed shocking; I guess where the person in front of you disapproves your actual self, the best option is to move on.

Coming out to family is perhaps one of the most difficult things in the world. Though they are supposed to be the closest ones in our lives, yet coming out to them seems to be the toughest, perhaps because we're too scared about being pushed aside by our own people, perhaps we're too sensitive about the reactions of our close ones.

I'm still not out to my family, I still couldn't gather the courage to disclose about my gender identity. Though I'm pretty confident about myself, yet I believe my parents won't accept me the way I am. This feeling haunts me day and night, but there isn't a way I can get over it. Aren't many of you going through the same situation? Right now, I'm in quest of a strong reason against 'why should they listen to me?' The most relevant point, that I'm their child, isn't valid here. Honestly, I dread their reactions the most and it's really hard to live like a person, different from me.

My mother was aware that her child wasn't really feminine. It seemed as if she was pretty cool with her child being boyish, as they call it. She used to joke about it with other aunties which led me to believe she had no problem with it. To my surprise, after some months I discovered that it was her way of hiding her insecurity. Yes, she was insecure about her child's gender identity. Like most mothers, she was also insecure about how I'll be treated by the society if I came out as a masculine female. She was insecure about my existence as an individual who doesn't follow the usual gender norms. I preferred to wear gender neutral clothes and mild pastel shades while my mother started insisting that I should wear bold feminine colours, lots of jewelry and make up. I was even given a tutorial for feminine gender expressions!

For non-binary AFAB individuals, body dysphoria can be a major issue. I'm glad to tell you that I've never really been dysphoric about my body. I wasn't really uncomfortable about the feminine curvature but I was conscious enough not to highlight it. I prefer to wear shirts and trousers rather than clothes which highlight my curves. I am perfectly comfortable with the feminine physical changes, like menstruation, as long as no female "role" is expected from me. I prefer to have my hair cut short, which helps me to present myself as gender neutral.

I'm still struggling to find pronouns. Pronouns are indeed important for one's identity. My gender falls in the neutral Spectra with a little inclination towards female gender. I certainly do not prefer "she" but I haven't yet figured out the appropriate pronoun for me. I've gone through numerous articles, sought help from a number of online forums and finally concluded that "Xie" might be the best suited for me; but I'm still working on it. Like others, I, too, face difficulties when at a certain place, the only pronoun options available are "he" and "she". By virtue of birth, I do choose "she" but I really feel I can't relate it with myself. I'm happy to see many online social platforms are being inclusive about pronouns other than the prevalent ones, yet the need to make these pronouns more popular and common among the layman cannot be negated.

My gender identity never affected my sexuality or romantic identity. I've always identified myself as homoromantic asexual and I do not feel, being non binary has ever made me rethink about my sexuality!

To be more precise, I should say my gender identity is "Non Binary Demi Girl", that is, I do not belong to the prevalent gender norms. I am basically gender neutral with partially inclined to my feminine side. However I do not include myself within the Trans spectrum. I belong to the "gender neutral but somewhat feminine" spectrum.

The journey of discovering myself gave me a sense of completeness. It gave me confidence and contentment. I felt more connected to myself. It evoked in me a feeling of utmost ecstasy. All this time, I felt trapped by an identity I can't relate to. Now I feel I've finally broken free. From the person I was bound to be, I am gradually transforming to the one I wanted to be.

Here's my message to all my fellow non binary people. The first step towards a healthy life is accepting yourself. You are not different, you are unique and you are one of us. For once, do stand in front of the mirror and ask yourself who you are. The answer might startle you, yet for sure, you'll get to know yourself better. There are a lot of hurdles in the outer world, the main being non acceptance by the people around. Just remember, the people around are always suspicious about what they've never seen. When people get your gender wrong, being rebellious isn't likely to fetch you anything. All you have to realize and make others believe is that you're a human; you're one of them and want to be treated alike. Coping up needs a lot of mental strength. Whenever your confidence hits the floor, whenever you need help, go ahead. Get connected. Someday you might as well end up helping your fellow people. There was a day when I had been desperately looking for help, but now I have my own support group. Always remember, You Are Valid. While the closet might be a safe place for you, it's certainly not the suitable one. Start the quest, you might be lucky enough to find a Narnia inside the closet!

Alyssa Hillary
Age – 25
One of agender, androgyne, or
fuck-it-autism-is-too-a-gender
depending on when you ask.

9: Am I confused? Are you?
2017

When I was four, I quit ballet because it was an all-girls' class. What did I know then, that I forgot for far too long?

When I was nine and ten, I heard that boys had "cooties." I was confused. What were "cooties," why did only boys have them, and was I supposed to care? I *did* understand that if I sat at a table full of boys, I wouldn't be followed by anyone who said the boys had "cooties." That was sufficient.

When I was eleven, my chest grew. I didn't want anyone to know I had a chest. It wasn't supposed to be there. That was dysphoria. That still is dysphoria. How long until I can get rid of these lumps of fat?

When I was twelve, I got my first period. I mistook it for diarrhea coming out the wrong hole, because it was brown. (So, I was confused.) I hated the feeling of pads, and how they never stuck to my underwear but how they *always* managed to stick to my legs. That wasn't dysphoria. It was just a pain in the ass (or, well, the abdomen.) Tampons helped.

I think I was still twelve when a friend told me I wasn't "really" a girl, one summer day at the local lake. He didn't know he was right. (He knows now.)

When I was thirteen, my voice dropped. It never occurred to me that this wasn't "supposed" to happen. (Was that a point of confusion?) My voice was changing, and that was fine. Really, the only issue with my becoming a low tenor instead of a low alto was that the choir director wasn't quite sure what to do with that. After all, girls didn't sing tenor. (I wasn't a girl. They didn't know that.)

When I was fourteen and fifteen and sixteen and seventeen, I was *absent* from high school more days than I wore pants (The numbers were something like ten and eight, respectively. Six of the absences were for math competitions.) I lived in skirts and dresses. That was how to be a girl, right? I was *definitely* confused about this whole gender thing. None of the *actual* girls wore skirts that much. I sat at a lunch table that was entirely boys, except for me. I joined *tenor bass choir* my junior year. But that didn't matter, right? I wore skirts, so I was a girl, right? (Wrong.)

Tenor bass choir *did* matter, and I wasn't a girl. The prerequisite for that class reads (or read, I haven't checked since I graduated): "Male members of concert chorus in good standing are eligible to audition for tenor bass choir." I wasn't a male member of concert chorus in good standing. Why didn't I audition for treble choir? That was for *female* members of concert chorus in good standing. That's what I was, right? (Wrong. My skirts helped everyone make that mistake, though. Also, I *did* audition for treble choir. Three times. I was cut three times because *I'm a tenor*.)

Let's also remember that time my senior year when I asked the choir director, "For the purposes of this ensemble, what gender will I be tomorrow night at 7pm?" The real question was, should I wear the same uniform as everyone else in tenor bass choir, the ensemble I sang in, or should I wear the same uniform as the girls, the gender I was supposedly part of. I wore the men's uniform, like the other members of my ensemble. Was I confused about my gender? Were they?

When I was twenty, I wrote about the erasure of Queer Autistic people for *Criptiques*. I read so much that year, both academic and personal. Autistic concepts of gender were called a *copia*, whatever that meant. Autistic people compared asking about their gender to asking how many miles per gallon an electric bike got. I understood the part where some of us didn't "get" gender in the neurotypical way (Jack, 2012). Was that why I was confused? I did my research, and then I added this at the top of my essay:

> Writing this, I realized: Why do I feel the need, writing academically, to distance myself from my identities? Why is this expected in academia? So I won't do

so. I say "we," not "they" for groups I am a member of. I will not feign the distanced impartiality of an outside observer: it would be erasing my own Queer Autistic voice to do so! (Hillary, 2014, p. 121).

I didn't *quite* know I was nonbinary yet, but I knew I wasn't cishet and I knew academia liked to claim a distanced lack of bias when no such thing was really possible. We are all informed by who we are and what we have experienced. Only some of us consider what that means for our work.

When I was twenty one, I finally understood why I had always felt "off" in women's spaces, why I had never adjusted to the lumps of tissue on my chest that aren't supposed to be there, why messages about what girls should and shouldn't do had always sort of ... bounced. I wasn't "different from the other girls." (Though, to be fair, I was pretty different. I'm autistic. It happens.) *I wasn't a girl. I wasn't a woman. I was nonbinary.*

I was still twenty one when a stranger grabbed my chest in broad daylight, on a well-traveled road. *He* thought I was a woman. I already knew better, but that didn't protect me, couldn't protect me.

When I was twenty two, I started using "they" pronouns for my introductions and bios. I started with my work as an assistant in an online classroom. Updating my introduction by changing every "she" to "they" and then hitting "send" was surprisingly nerve-wracking. Once the change was accepted, students asking if I was a boy or a girl was ... less scary. The answer was no. I was not a boy or a girl.

I wasn't. I'm still not. But people still treat me as a woman. That's one of the weird things about being nonbinary while also being read as a woman. *I* know I'm not a woman. The people who are sexist assholes towards women? *They* don't know I'm not a woman. *They* don't know they're confused about my gender. They are confused, though – they're pretty sure I'm a woman. Even the people who are merely trying to be chivalrous don't quite seem to get that I'm not a lady, and that treating me as one *is* misgendering.

Explaining that I'm not a woman – that I'm not actually in the category they hate so much, or so want to protect – wouldn't be the right defense anyways. When people say I shouldn't do something because I'm a girl, or a lady, or a female, or a woman, "I'm not a woman" is a technically correct response. That doesn't make it the *right* response. No more than "I'm not mentally ill" is the *right* response to people who argue that trans or nonbinary people are all mentally ill.

I may not be a woman, but I'm not leaving them in the dust.

One answer to being told what women shouldn't do is, "Fuck you." Another is, "Women should do whatever they so please." (I'm not going to claim womanhood, even if I'm not going to make pointing out that I'm *not* one my main argument.) A third is "I'll give your opinion all the consideration it deserves." (Specifying that *no* consideration is deserved is optional here.)

One answer to being told that I must be mentally ill because I am nonbinary is, "Fuck you." Another is, "And I have brown eyes. Not sure how that's relevant, though." A third is "I'll give your opinion all the consideration it deserves." (Specifying that *no* consideration is deserved remains optional.)

One answer to being told that I'm not really nonbinary, just autistic, is, "Fuck you." Another is, "Why not both?" A third is "I'll give your opinion all the consideration it deserves." (I probably will specify that this means *no* consideration.)

I could also tell them that yes, my gender is autistic! That's the point! They wouldn't get it, and they wouldn't care. They might not even know they're confused. They'd be pretty sure I was confused, though!

Are *you* confused about my gender? Don't worry, so am I. As long as we recognize that things can be both confusing and real, we'll be fine.

10: Just Me
2017

I remember when I started transitioning wishing more than once that I had been born a boy, instead of the baby girl that my mother brought home from the hospital. It's been about ten years since I started my gender identity journey and my view on gender, along with many things, has changed. I no longer wish I was born male but instead embrace the experiences I had because I was born a cis-gender female. The more I'm viewed as male, as "one of the guys", the less I want to be seen as a "man".

When I started transitioning I would search and find discussion boards about "how to pass", to be viewed as male. What haircut would help you pass, clothing, accessories, glasses, shoes... There were threads about how to sit and take up more space "like a man", how to walk "manly", and even how to go to the bathroom "like a man". At first, I started following most of suggestions I could find to appear more "manly" while I waited for the testosterone to do its magic. I wore button down shirts and layers over my binder to try to further hide my breasts; I smiled less and tried to talk more assertively.

After checking the mirror every day for what seemed liked forever I remember being ecstatic when I noticed my first peach fuzz of facial hair start coming in. There were other changes that I was not as happy about but I felt that I could not really complain, that it was just part of "becoming a man". I started on what seemed to be the "typical" dose of testosterone for those just starting transitioning and wanting to see changes come fairly quickly. At first my injections were every two weeks, but I fairly quickly changed to once a week after noticing the mood changes that came as the testosterone level would start to fade after it peaked a bit too quickly.

Once I had been on testosterone for a bit of time I started regularly "passing" without a problem, although the fear and anxiety of being "discovered" was always high for me. I had a hysterectomy, legally changed my name, and moved cross-country with my wife at the time and step-daughter. Besides the director of HR no staff at my new job knew that I was Trans*, and for a brief period of time it stayed that way, which was a new experience to me as I had never been "stealth" before. It felt somewhat uncomfortable being "stealth", always having to be mindful when I talked about my past.

After that I tried to find jobs where I felt that I would be accepted when, and if, I disclosed my Trans* identity to my co-workers. There were some jobs where I would "come out" quickly and others where I wouldn't "come out" right away, or just to a few people. Before starting to transition I had already spent about ten years working in and around kitchens while identifying as female. In this experience I thought that I was already fully aware of the level of toxic masculinity that existed in kitchens, along with everywhere else, but once I started being viewed as "one of the guys" I realized that the toxic masculinity ran deeper than I had thought.

Really, what is masculinity? Why is it so often toxic? What does it mean to "be a man"? In kitchens it seemed like often masculinity was determined by things like how fast you could chop onions without crying, how many cases of potatoes you could carry at once, or if you wince when you burn your hand on the grill. In one kitchen a male supervisor would proudly brag about making culinary interns cry and sometimes drop out of their internships, is this masculinity? There almost always seems to be this competitiveness among men, which is different than the competitiveness that comes out amongst women, even just walking down the street can seem like a competition for two men. If they're on the same path and when doesn't move they'll bump into each other, which often can result in a fight. Does fighting a stranger who bumped into you or cut you off in traffic make you a "real man"?

Early on in my gender identity journey I would only wear certain colors like greens and blues because pinks and purple because were "girly" colors, and I didn't want to "out myself". However, at some point I started wearing whatever colors I wanted because colors don't have genders and I'm going to wear clothes that I like the color of. Maybe it was the confidence I gained in finally having top surgery two years ago, or perhaps the experiences I had being seen as "one of the guys" but I realized that although at first I wanted nothing more than to fit in the 'male' box, it was not the box for me either.

Why is it that even before We as human beings are born we are already being shoved into these predetermined boxes? Before a baby is even born often parents have "gender reveal parties" complete with a cake that is either pink or blue inside, so they can cut into it and "discover" the gender of the baby. A pink cake will mean dolls, tutus, and encouragement to be nurturing and "sensitive". A blue cake will mean toy guns, blocks, encouraged to play "rough", and only to express certain emotions.

At some point I realized that I was starting to fit a bit too well into a box that I wasn't sure I even wanted to be in. It felt like the toxicity of masculinity was trying, maybe starting to seep in, and it was something that I did not want. If to be part of "one of the guys" you either have to remain silent, or brush it off "locker room talk", when other men talk about "grabbing women by the pussy"; I don't want to be "one of the guys". If to be a "real man" you have to look at other people like they are objects to be owned, to the point where other people notice the "inspection" you do with your eyes, then I don't want to be a "real man".

I don't want to be put into any box. Why does my gender need a label anyway, especially when society designates those labels? A society founded on exploitation, exuding patriarchy, swelling to the brim with systematic racism, and institutionalized misogyny. I just want to be me, if being me means no longer having breasts, having a low-level of testosterone, and sporting a beard, why does that have to put me in the 'male' box. I'm done with boxes, I just want to be me.

Emil Eichelberger
Age – 26
Genderqueer

11: Progress Not Perfection
2017

I was 19 when I first heard the terms "non-binary" and "genderqueer." For me, it signified the beginning of a new life; a life with understanding. I could now look back on my existence while picking out the bits and pieces that had never quite made sense when held up to the mirror of my peers and analyze them with fresh eyes. But, perhaps more importantly than that, I could now live my life knowing that I was not alone. There were other people who felt hurtful confusion whenever school activities were separated by binary gender. Other people who squirmed in their chairs and completely dissociated during family life and sex education classes.

It wasn't long after I had discovered this word, this community, this sense of self that I became terrified that I would lose it all. I had had various forms of dysphoria prior to realizing that I was non-binary. All of this exploration of myself seemed to amp it up to a level that was unhealthy for me to live with. And yet, I continued to stuff it down further and further. The expectations that I had placed upon myself dictated that I needed to stay away from medical interventions that could have alleviated my dysphoria. I could not have both hormone replacement therapy and a non-binary identity. Starting testosterone would mean surrendering the identity I had fought to find.

This left me in a sad, dark place. A place where I was letting outside forces impose upon me who I was. It was a place that took away my decisions and my choices. I emotionally checked out and distanced myself from my body. It has been a fairly recent development that I have been able to reclaim the oneness that I now experience in relating my gender identity to myself.

The moment of clarity that I had in realizing that I had lost sight of what it meant to be inside my skin happened at my four-week post op appointment following top surgery. I was sitting in my surgeon's parking lot after having the last of the ace bandages removed and realized that, for the first time in living memory, I could feel the fabric of my car seat pressing against my back. There wasn't a binder or any other compression material sitting between the nylon and my skin. I experienced utter completeness and suddenly understood that I had spent years of my life contemplating what the end goal of my transition should look like instead of focusing on the journey that it had presented to me.

All too often, I feel as though I am an intruder whenever I enter any space that is designed for non-binary folks because I "pass" so well. On the other hand, my experience with several trans inclusive spaces has been that these places often drift into a more binary focus leaving me feeling as though there is no word or identity that truly encompasses my existence. The time that I spend in my head mulling these things over always comes back to that first word that fit me so well when I first starting putting myself together: genderqueer.

The meaning has evolved for me in the years I have spent contemplating my connection to it. Today, it means something that, on a certain level, it has always meant for me: my relationship with my gender has and always will be queer. It is non-normative in nature. It is subversive in its very existence. And, it is never inherently male or female. I am, and always will be, a working progress as opposed to a perfect introspective being that must know precisely who they are at any given moment.

My transition has been more of an opportunity for growth and development than a fixed route with a final destination. I have been given the chance to do work on and inside of myself that other people don't get the chance to do. There are certain parts of myself I do not take lightly such as the fact that I can walk into any space and be immediately perceived as a white, cis male. However, there are parts of myself that I have learned that I must have more compassion and more flexibility for including my inner sense of gender. No matter what path I decide to take in life, it does not have to be perfect or make complete sense to everyone else around me. But, it does have to be my choice. For me, the freedom of identifying as non-binary as always, if not anything else, presented me with choices. And, for that, I can be proud.

Gyps Curmi
Age – 60
Gender-diverse, trans*, non-binary,
gender non-conforming

12: Free to be Me
2017

I'm four. Dad is leaving for two weeks with his mates in the army reserve. He did his duty, moving us from the city into our housing commission way out at Sevo. We've got no furniture to speak of and the winter winds are screaming like raucous ghosts through the gaps in the floorboards.

I stand outside on the porch, shivering in my thin over-coat and breathing steam into my mittened fingers. I wish we were all inside huddling around the gas fire in the lounge room instead. But I have to see him off. He's my Dad. My hero. I want to be just like him when I grow up.

'Look after the women, son, you're the man of the house now.'

I stand at attention, puffing out my chest and grinning at his confidence in me. Then I see he's talking to my three-year-old brother. The poor baby clinging to our mother's hand, his face turned into her skirts for warmth and crying from the cold. How can Dad ask that of Jimmy Junior?

'I'll look after them, Dad! I'm the oldest.'

I wait for Dad's praise. But my words echo hollowly into the misty silence. He doesn't even look at me as he gets in his car. Maybe he doesn't hear me.

'I'll look after them Dad.'

I call out louder this time, but he just turns on his motor, gives a quick wave and drives away. The fog swallows him.

I don't understand.

I learn that Jimmy's penis makes him special. Dad loves him. Wants 'father and son' time with him that doesn't include me. Even though everyone says they 'should be the other way round'. Jimmy, who'd rather be wearing Mum's high heels and bright red lipstick, has to be cajoled up into the 'manhole,' up into the torch lit dark of the ceiling. Jimmy is terrified of spiders and has redback nightmares for months. I'm forbidden. I ball my hands into fists. Jimmy does nothing to earn Dad's affection. I'm so jealous I punch Jimmy when I get a chance. And I keep fighting with him for years. I don't hate him. I just want Dad to see me too.

Mum finally gives up dressing me in scratchy frocks and telling me how to sit and walk.

'I'm going to marry Dela.' She's the girl down the road. I'm seven now but I first meet her when we are four. She's a month older (so she's always telling me to have respect for my elders). She's swinging on her front gate, looking like a cupie doll. Mum tells me to keep my head down and keep walking,

'Sticks and stones' she whispers. But we stop to talk when Dela's mother hails her over. Even though Dela acts shy and like she wants nothing to do with me that day, she's soon at my back door, snot dribbling in runnels 'til she sniffs it up or licks it away, wanting to play. (Mum thinks she's germy and I should stay away, but she lets me anyway).

'You can't marry a girl,' Dad says when I tell him.
'Why not?'
'It's just the way it is.'
'That's no reason.'
'You can't have babies without a man,' he says, making it clear.
'You don't need to have babies to be married. Look at Uncle John and Aunty Maeve'.

Again that silence.

I'm a 'tomboy' and it's ok. Everyone says I'll 'grow out of it.' I know I won't so I keep modelling myself on my Dad and the older boys in my street.

I know it's no biggy I don't have a penis (which are pretty weird and floppy, and a bit ugly too). I'm just a boy with a vagina.

One day, I see a little boy wailing on his front lawn.

'Big boys don't cry.'

I do him a favour, letting him know.

I run around the neighbourhood in tough bare feet, stubbies and a naked chest. I climb trees and catch blue-tongues and bearded dragons. Dela likes to join in. But she likes to scream like a girl sometimes and play with Barbies. Which is boring.

Come summer, we compare tans. This is the one thing I can do better than her and I'm proud of it.

'You're the wrong shade,' she announces, pulling her arm away to admire it. 'You're not a lovely golden brown like me.'

She's learning from her Mum who likes to taunt me for having a 'touch of the tar brush,' and carries on about 'dirty lazy wogs' who should 'go home' stealing their jobs.

'But Aunty Kaitlin, you're talking about my Mum. You're talking about me.' I want her to see what she's doing.

'Oh, but you're different.'

96

Like that makes it ok.

I tell Mum and she preens to think she's different. But I look in the mirror and see there is no difference but skin. The way Dela's Mum talks and acts is like we don't have feelings. Aren't as real. Aren't quite human. Her games and names hurt.

I hate my traitorous body. My nipples bud but I defy them, as I walk shirtless up to the corner shop. No-one even notices, let alone says anything, but I feel so ashamed I never go out that way again.

When I felt saddest, I used to run through a litany of potential boys' names I could use when I grow up, but nothing consoles me now. I can't deny it anymore. They're right after all. I am a girl. My self-confidence leaks away. I wish I was dead.

'Come out, Dad has something important to say.' Mum cajoles me from my bedroom door, big smile on her face.

So we crowd around the dining room table, excited for the news.

'This is a very special day.' Dad announces. Jimmy and I catch each other's eyes, wondering. Annie has begun menstruating.' Dad beams at me. 'She is a woman now.' He smiles approvingly. Like I finally did something worthwhile.

My ears ring and I blush, horrified. He's parading my

shame in front of the whole family. I shoot Mum daggers. I can't believe she told him. How dare she lure me out of my bloody huddled misery for this. They want to celebrate with coffee and cake. I feel sick.

I cry for a week from the shame, even though 'big boys don't cry'. It doesn't matter anymore. I'm a girl. And womanhood comes with a vengeance. Two weeks of cramps and hot water bottles, and bleeding like a stuck pig, then two weeks reprieve, before it starts all over again. Year after year. I hate it. Hate myself.

Being a 'woman' doesn't stop Dad beating me when I'm sixteen. So much for 'men never hit women.' His patriarchal double standards.

I don't want to be just like him anymore.

I try to be a girl. Even wear a dress to a school dance feeling like I'm in drag. I 'practice' kissing with Dela and try dating boys. But I don't want to fuck them – don't want to get pregnant – and all they want is a fuck, not me. Dad says you have to be a virgin when you get married. But I lost mine on the bar of a boys' bike years ago.

I leave 'home' at eighteen. Find I don't have to use my fists to survive. People speak to me 'cause they want to know me. It's not just a prelude to bashing me. I still don't really trust them, keep waiting for the first punch. Until they invite me for a joint on the roof at morning tea and I let my guard down.

David Bowie and Patti Smith show me androgyny. I love

the freedom of ambiguity. Boys with their long blow-dried locks and girls in loose fitting men's shirts. Music with lyrics that matter and punk rhythms. I don't know any 'virgins' here in the city.

I go on the pill and join in the fun. Fucking anybody that catches my eye for a one-night-stand of dancing, mandrax and grog. And it is fun. Not really me, but it staves off the wrist slitting black dog.

I long for some fairy tale happy ending and think I find it in the arms of a butch, non-monogamous, Ducati riding dyke. But it's just a whirlwind heroin romance that ends all too soon. In depression.

There's an empty space inside me that never fills. I'm in my twenties, and look for meaning in the beds of overall wearing, man-hating feminist-lesbians. It's a fit of sorts. But their white, 'classless' simplistic politics don't include me. And it's too easy just to hate anyone with a dick = patriarchy.

I discover uni in my late thirties. I always thought I was too dumb to do anything but work in the uni kitchen. But mature age entry gets me a degree in visual arts.
A cross-discipline unit called *Borderlands* starts me on a second degree in identity politics and cultural studies. I find words for the things I feel, and people in these borderlands with stories like mine. Finally, I'm beginning to find my place. In a presentation for *Gender, Sexuality and Identity* I show a *YouTube* video of a young man documenting his gender transition. I'm blown away that it's

even possible... But I'm too old. If only I was young again.

When I give up looking, I do find the partner of my dreams. I'm in my late forties, so who would have thought? I ask Dad to honour me, walking me down the aisle.

The silence grows.

'I can't.' He clears his throat. 'It's against my (newly adopted) Christian values.'

Kelly isn't Dela, but she is a woman.

Dad's Christian values don't stop him watching 'Asian girls' paedophilia or gay male porn or asking me to delete his internet history, because the viruses are clogging up his system. Just like his prostate.

I used to adore him. I wanted to be just like him. I'm starting to realise I don't even like him.

Dad dies. A slow, writhing, painful death. It's horrible. Horrible. I wouldn't wish it on my worst enemy. Then he's gone. A huge load lifts from me. I don't need his approval anymore. He can't judge me or condemn me. He can't hurt me anymore. I'm free. Finally. Free to be me.

I have to transition. Now.

But I need to wait because I'm going back to Malta to see my old people there one more time. It will break my heart if they reject me because I'm trans.

I can't wait. I'm fifty-seven. I need my body to reflect who I am. If they love me they will love me anyway, and if they don't, so be it. If I wait any longer I might be dead.

Deciding and starting are two different things. Where's the information? The support? How do I even begin? No professionals in this rural place know. I join *Facebook* support groups for trans and non-binary people and question from their borderlands. Inform myself. Negotiating the hoops and educating GPs is challenging, but finally, I begin. I find others in the community who are, or have, transitioned to talk to. And surprisingly, most of them are old too.

One year on T. I have Kelly, strong support systems and an endocrinologist who 'gets it.' Mum mostly remembers to use my pronouns, and Jimmy compares his patchy beard with the fuzz on my cheeks. The person I have always been is emerging. My second pimply puberty at sixty. I still have a long way to go and I will never 'pass' as or *be* 'male.' I've lived all my life in a female body. I won't deny those experiences. Injustices. Discriminations. But I have, also, always been male. I am both. I am they. The person I am is in the mirror.

Jo Smiley
Age – 25
Nonbinary (agender)

13: The Path to Gender Neutrality

2017

Being nonbinary is a long and often difficult road for anyone to walk, regardless of what gender we were assigned at birth. It can be hard to figure ourselves out. It can take a really long time for us to find any resources whatsoever. Like other LGBTQ and gender non-conforming people, we face discrimination, bigotry, and violence. For me, the biggest problem was that it took forever for me to even admit I was nonbinary in the first place.

When I was born and the doctor said those three words, "It's a girl," a huge part of my life was decided for me. My parents dressed me in floral print dresses and lace, and gave me a really feminine name that ran in the family, and probably showed me off to their friends as their adorable "little baby girl." Because of this label, "girl," I became overly attached to everything having to do with femininity. I was a "girly girl," so to speak. Even after I started dressing myself, I wore dresses and lace and drew flowers on things a lot of the time. As a child, I played with dolls, and I told people my favorite color was pink because I thought I had no choice in that matter. Really. I acted surprised when people didn't automatically know what my favorite color was, and I would tell them "uh, it's pink, duh! I'm a girl, aren't I?"

Of course, I played with Legos and Hotwheels too, and once I carved a Pinewood Derby car out of a block of wood and took part in a local Cub Scouts troop's race. Still, I was hyper-aware that all of these things were coded masculine. They were supposed to be "boy things." So, whenever I did them, I made sure to insist to everyone watching that I was still "girly." I carved the Pinewood Derby car in a slender, curvy shape and painted roses on the side of it. I probably wore pink to the race. I didn't want to be seen as a tomboy, because I was worried people might treat me differently if I didn't conform to the strictest of gender stereotypes.

Looking back on that, I think I was holding on to femininity so tightly because deep down, I knew I was somehow different from the others, and above all else, I just wanted to fit in.

I was in high school when I started calling myself a feminist. With that label, I felt suddenly free. It was an identity that allowed me to do whatever I wanted, whether or not that thing was considered feminine. I changed my favorite color to purple, then blue, then green, and I started wearing pants more often, and that felt radical to me. I rejoiced in my sudden ability to choose for myself, and to wear the clothing that felt comfortable to me.

Still, there was no doubt in my mind that I was a girl. I had been assigned that way, and I still had no idea that I was allowed to change that part of me.

In 2010, I graduated from high school and left my tiny Kentucky town behind in favor of a tiny Indiana town which was not much different. The difference was that the Indiana town had a college in it, and that college had a larger number of openly gay and trans people than my high school had. I started listening to more of their coming out stories, and declared myself to be an "ally" for LGBT rights. I threw myself into their movement and felt welcomed by them, and found community with them. And when I spoke to more of the trans students, I began to realize that the gender marker on a birth certificate has nothing whatsoever to do with the way a person feels on the inside. For the first time, I began to question my gender identity.

I've heard other nonbinary and trans people tell their stories, and in many of them, this is the point where they say "I discovered who I was and I never looked back!" But that is not my story. Even after I realized that I don't have to identify with the writing on my birth certificate, it took me several years to find the right descriptive words to explain what I was feeling.

On one hand, I really liked hanging out with the LGBT community, and I felt that I had something in common with them that I couldn't describe. There was an instant connection that had not been there in most of my high school friendships. But on the other hand, there was a perpetual stream of people online telling me not to "abandon femininity," and saying I would be a "bad feminist" if I "decided not to be a woman." While I know that's a BS argument now, back then, they got under my skin. And anyway, I was actually very proud of my femininity still. I was painting myself as a bold woman, a femme fatale, a warrior archetype like Buffy or Xena. I idolized them and I wanted to be like them. So, the result of my first bout of questioning was to decide I must still be a cisgender woman after all.

Besides that, I still didn't have any nonbinary role models. There were plenty of trans people I had become familiar with, but no nonbinary people that I knew of yet. I still hadn't heard that term. In my head back then, to be trans meant to switch from female to male or vice versa. Even still, the binary dictated all.

In 2014, I questioned my gender again. This time, it happened because I noticed that I was taking on more roles that seemed both feminine and masculine. I had several masculine traits that were coming to the forefront of my personality more often. Again, I thought about being trans, and wondered if I might be a trans man. But after only a weekend of this, I decided that I just plain did not feel like a man. I ignored the fact that I didn't feel like a woman either, and the fact that assigning binary identities to random personality traits is weird. I decided that I must still be cis.

I didn't fully separate myself from that cis identity until the following year, when I went on a Christmas road trip with my sister and her nonbinary fiancé. We met up with family at a resort in Virginia, since one of my cousins was getting married there, and we spent a long weekend together. Over that weekend, we teamed up with my other cousin (who is also nonbinary) and explored the resort. It was over that weekend that something finally struck a chord within me.

I felt a camaraderie with them that went beyond just family bonds. It was like the connection I had felt with the LGBT group at college, only this one was stronger. This time, there were two openly nonbinary people involved, and I suddenly had an example to go on. I was also hyper-aware that I was the "only cis person" in this group of four (my sister being trans), and for the first time, I felt awkward about that label. I felt like I didn't want it to apply to me, that I wanted to scream something different about my life. For the first time, thinking about the word "cisgender," I just felt wrong.

Over the next few months, I thought things over a lot. I sought out nonbinary blogs and found people who could give me a better understanding of the terms and issues involved. I labeled myself "genderfluid" at first, because a part of me was still tied to femininity. I told people that my gender fluctuated between "female" and "agender." Still, I felt awkward about everything female. It felt too much like I was just going along with the same old stereotypes I had clung to as a child. A few months later, I abandoned the genderfluid label and came out as nonbinary.

Several things changed when I came out. First, I started trying to present myself more androgynously so that people would stop assuming I'm a woman on first glance. Then, I stopped feeling as welcome in some of the women's rights groups I had been a part of previously. Their talk of "You're a woman, you're one of us! We don't care how you dress!" had been empowering before, but now it just felt like misgendering. Don't get me wrong: I'm still a feminist, but I choose my organizations very carefully now.

Since coming out, I have taken several steps to make myself feel more comfortable with my identity and with my body. I cut my hair shorter, and I started going by a gender-neutral nickname. I wear neutral clothing, and I use a sports bra to bind my chest flatter so that my breasts won't "give me away" so to speak. I also changed the pronouns I want people to refer to me by: it took a lot of explaining, but my immediate family agreed to say "they." To help people remember, I got a button from a booth at Pride which reads "they/them/theirs," and when I'm wearing it, it really helps people to understand that I am not a cisgender woman.

I still get dysphoria, even with these strategies in place. That's always going to happen, I think. No matter how tightly I bind my chest, or how short my hair is, I'm going to occasionally see myself in the mirror after a shower and think "society thinks you are a woman," and it is going to make me feel uncomfortable. But knowing a lot of trans and nonbinary people has helped me learn how to deal with that when it happens. My most important coping mechanisms are psychological, and they just involve reminding myself that just because I have breasts doesn't mean I'm a woman. Everyone has breasts, just some people's are bigger than others. Some men have bigger breasts than me.

All things considered, I am very happy that I finally found the nonbinary community, and I'm incredibly relieved that the larger LGBT community welcomes me as one of their own. I'm glad that I can connect with people online who understand the issues I face, who are facing the same ones, and who can offer advice if I need help figuring something out. And I'm proud of my identity. It took me a while to get here, but now that I'm here, considering all the effort it took, I think I have the right to be proud.

14: The Long Way Around
2017

I'm 39 years old, married, no kids. I'm a writer, artist, thinker, and general p.i.t.a.

You may call me Kai.

I was born in 1978 in Duesseldorf, Germany. I grew up in a tiny village near Cologne. It was a town so small, it had only one road, one bakery, one teensy grocery store and a pub with a theater in the basement. There was also a castle, a Renaissance style church, and an ancient Roman tower that smelled like graveyard.

It was picturesque and boring.

In retrospect, I was already different as a child. I preferred playing outside in rain and dirt. I disregarded dolls. I loved wearing pants and petticoats, preferably together. I still do. I always came home covered in mud with gum in my hair and scratches all over me. I was wild, because nothing was expected of me, yet.

I was the younger of two children. My brother, six years older, was my hero until I reached puberty. Our relationship then began to deteriorate, eventually to die an untimely death.

There was never a grand explanation as to what it was that made me different, other than that I simply was.

When I got older, I failed to fit in with either boys or girls. I've always been hesitant to trust people and ended up with a mere few hand-picked friends.

My interests were influenced by what was expected of me and not what I really wanted. I did what I thought was expected of a young girl, though I was still different and often perceived as an oddity.

I remember feeling as if I was wearing a permanent mask.

I wrote dark poetry that gained me the praise of my teachers, but not their understanding. I was never myself, but a shallow copy of what society wanted me to be.

Back then, the idea of being transgender was not a hot topic. Researching it prior to the internet was difficult, if not impossible. I wasn't even familiar with the concept until my late teens when I had my own TV to watch documentaries at night. Even then, being transgender was not something that was openly talked about unless you were part of the community.

I was not.

I tried to fit in with the only community I knew. My friends, my school, my family. In time, I did what I'd learned best. I swallowed and suppressed the growing uneasiness, the feeling that I was just acting.

> Like a doll on strings that was moved
> by an invisible hand.

Getting my first period and seeing my breasts grow was a catastrophe.

I was knowledgeable enough to understand what was happening to me, but since I was a late bloomer, already 13-14 when my first menstruation arrived, I had hoped that it would never come and I would just stay genderless for the rest of my life. It was a silly little fantasy.

My father began touching me when I was twelve.

I do not wish to go into detail as it would only distract, but it continued for years and was a contributing factor to my abnormal need to keep up appearances. Pretending was the lifeblood of my family. I always knew that, but it became worse once I had to carry the burden of such a secret. I was further made to understand that the harmony of my family rested solely on my ability to shut my mouth and be a "good girl."

Long before the abuse, I began having a recurring dream.

I was different there. I was happiest when I saw myself as a person in-between. Not a man, not a woman, but a genderless individual. In my dream, my body was neither male or female. I had no breasts, my face was undefined by gender features. I had no penis. My silhouette could easily go either way. The person in my dream did not fit any role, any generally accepted idea of the binary in body or mind.

In time, this dream became my only refuge. It took me years to understand that I was suffering from depression and even more years to realize that the flares of intense self-hatred, and ideas of self-mutilation were dysphoria.

The idea of being FTM never crossed my mind. First, because I had no idea it existed and second, I didn't feel like a man. (I knew MTF, I wasn't completely oblivious.)

But I was certainly not a woman, not in my mind, not the way I felt. The only evidence of my womanhood was what was forced upon me.

I hated to be seen as a woman, but I pretended to be normal, because pretending was what I could do best.

I was the master actor.

Meeting my spouse was a blessing.

He accepted me the way I was, but that was a problem. I've never been who I really was.

I was so used to keeping up appearances, I didn't realize that I had become unstable. The master actor dominated my behavior, but my perception of what was expected had become warped. My reactions were exaggerated, dishonest, a reflection of the twisted caricature that I was. I didn't notice how I interacted with people. I didn't understand why my oldest friends turned away from me. I didn't realize that I was in the process of ruining my marriage.

I was puzzled why I still felt happiest in my dreams as a genderless individual.

There was a wall around my true self,
and I refused, unconsciously, to let them out.

We moved from Germany to my spouse's stomping grounds, the US, in 2007. We were hoping for a change, a better life and I think that, at least in my spouse's mind, there was hope that the distance from my family would make me free.

It didn't work, not for years.

Everything imploded three years ago. The big turning point that cracked the wall. I finally realized I was nothing but a crooked mask, overused and warped from years of abuse. I revealed my biggest secret to my spouse despite an overwhelming fear that he would not believe me. But he did. There wasn't an ounce of doubt in him.

A short while later, I realized that I've never been part of the binary. It took me almost my entire life to get to this point and I felt betrayed because I'd wasted so many years pretending. Years that I could have spent doing something, getting surgery, maybe hormones. Instead

I'd played "good girl."

But there was also a fear in the back of my mind that the idea of being agender was influenced by my abuse. I will not deny that it may have been a contributing factor, but it wasn't the reason for rejecting the binary.

If anything, the abuse caused me to become a better, more convincing actor. It forced me to bury the agender creature within myself.

It did not create it.
It had always been there. It just was never allowed to come out.

People always seek an explanation for what they do not understand. I struggled with myself about including the abuse in this story because I know what many people are going to assume from it.

"This person is broken. 'She' is just confused by the trauma."

Well, certainly, yes. I was broken.

The symptom of my trauma was not my gender identity, but the struggle to suppress it. My trauma caused me to play a woman when I was not.

The acceptance of who and what I really am is what is healing me. The agender me (they, them, themself) was hidden under a pile of baggage and surrounded by a wall my entire life. I was broken when I was playing along. I was confused when I could not understand and recognize myself in the mirror.

That day three years ago saved me and, ultimately, my marriage. My spouse and I have been working hard on my healing process since then. Our relationship has grown and continues to grow with each passing day. It's difficult at times. I have phases of deep depression, bouts of dysphoria, and also flashbacks and night-terrors. My spouse is always at my side.

My coming out to what remains of my German family, (my step-brother and step-father, plus a small group of friends,) was difficult because they had no idea what agender even means. My step-father still doesn't understand it, but he is happy when I'm happy and promised me all his support, so I'll leave it at that. He is in Germany, I'm in the US. I don't see any reason to confuse him any further when he can't talk to me in person.

My mother died 2012 after a six month long battle against pancreas cancer. She never lived to see me bloom.

Agender Kai, hidden deep within me for almost my entire life, finally overtook the actor. I am working on accepting myself the way I am but there are obstacles.

It appears that it is easier for society to accept transgender people as long as they stay within the binary. Breaking its boundaries by being an individual in-between or outside its limitations, seems to be repulsive even to some trans people.

The fact that we transition in half-steps, never go all the way and seek out the in-between is considered half-hearted, unworthy of consideration. To many, we're snowflakes wishing to be special.

That's a fine word: "Special." Sadly, it seems that people associate it with vanity nowadays. Almost as if it is a crime to be different.

We wish to stop wearing masks. Just as millions of trans-people before us, we also want to be accepted. Conformity is not healthy if it kills the spirit.

The binary is an invention, serving as means to classify the two biological sexes of the human race and assign roles to each.

Society indoctrinates a value: male - dominance, female - passivity.

Rule and obey.

Master and slave.

What is and what isn't male or female is not and was never decided by nature. It does not need such values.

Our biological sex does not define our gender. It merely assigns a role to our body (give seed, give birth,) not to our life. Gender is who we are.

I am agender even though I have a womb. I am agender even though my biological sex is female.

Thanks to modern science, we are now able to adjust our bodies.

Getting surgery and hormones to come closer to what we consider our true self is not mutilation.

It is creation.

As creatures capable of adaption, we have the hereditary right and duty to evolve from the infant human, restrained by arbitrary concepts.

Binary trans people are a prime example. They know they are not the sex they were born with.

Why then, is it so outlandish to insist that we do not belong to either side of the binary? We are not a threat. We are part of this world.

This is our life. There is no one better to decide what to do with it than ourselves. It took me decades to figure that out. Years of torment. No youth should have to go through that. We should evolve from our attachment to antiquated ideas and embrace the future, instead of fighting it.

15: Building Families
2017

One of my first memories as a child is my dad responding to a family member asking if he wasn't upset that my newborn younger sister wasn't a boy. "Then you'd have a boy and a girl, one of each!" said family member cheerfully proclaimed. As if such an observation was some epiphany that dad hadn't realized previously. Dad calmly came back with "Why would I need a son? I have Lis." But in the car driving home from the family get-together, he groused repeatedly about what message the curious aunt or uncle (I don't remember which- there were a lot of both in our family) was sending to me with a question like that. "Who in hell cares whether they have sons or daughters? All that matters is the kids are healthy."

Dad's affirmation of me as equal, and of my gender as irrelevant, was true in his actions as well as his words. In our house, once my sister was on the scene, we basically split the parents between ourselves. Mom and Kim were constantly together, in part because Kim was

121

younger and mom was the primary caregiver; in part because they just got along better than mom and I. The two of them had similar interests, similar personalities, and similar looks. Meanwhile, dad and I would be paired for most of the time. While mom and Kim shopped and cleaned, dad and I did yardwork and I helped him in the shop, sorting parts, holding things, hammering or using the screwdriver as needed. Mom would protest when somebody said it – she thought it was insulting for some reason – dad and I looked similar enough for me to be called "Little Kenny" by many of dad's friends and coworkers. Mom had had numerous miscarriages prior to my birth and a couple more between my sister and I. Dad's emphasis on the health of the child as foremost in importance was in part due to those ten years trying to bring a single, healthy pregnancy to fruition, he was not some radical feminist male ally in rural Ohio in the early eighties (was that even a thing?).

No matter which parent I was with, I never identified as feminine. If I was stuck going to mother-daughter banquets at church, I was the obnoxious child tearing down the halls, sliding on my knees, and crawling under the table instead of going around. Hair was an endless struggle. I would refuse to take care of it if mom tried to make me grow it out, we'd fight when she tried to brush or comb it, I'd cut it off and she'd either have it fixed professionally or not depending on her mood, and the cycle would start all over. Clothing was only a problem around special occasions. We weren't well off financially, so I usually had hand me down clothes, and my older cousins were mostly boys. But come Christmas and Easter, a new dress or fancy Scottie dog sweater would appear and I would either resign myself to the indignity of frills or fight like hell against the monstrosities. In school, I frequently ended up being the last kid assigned to a group, mostly because of my inability to respond correctly to cues. Teachers would have girls line up on one side, and boys on the other, and I'd be sitting in my seat happily ignoring what was going on around me, or trying to remember which role I supposed to play in this game. Nearly all of my friends were boys, and I really didn't understand those foreign creatures who *liked* long hair, dresses, bows, and lace, even if I was supposedly one of them.

When I heard the term "tomboy" I had at least had a name that was closer to how I felt. It conveyed that I was not one of those delicate flowers, at least. That was a bit of a comfort, but it still didn't feel perfectly at ease. Dad died when I was 14, and suddenly I was thrust into the role of "man of the house" but as a kid and as what everybody assumed was a girl. Mom's alcoholism, an abusive step father, and my own drug use kept me busy until my 18th birthday, when I signed papers and bought my first home to escape the bullshit. I lost myself in so many ways for those years, I'm not going to try and lead you through that morass, but skip forward to when I met my current husband and started to realize again that I was worth looking for.

It wasn't until I was 24 and pregnant with my son that my body felt vaguely like my own. Maybe not like I belonged in this body entirely, but at least I was putting these corporeal parts to good use. He was an unplanned pregnancy. We had married when I was 21, and after a few years I went off birth control because the pill was absolutely horrendous. I hated it. I was pregnant in less than two months off contraceptives. My husband and I were trying to not get pregnant – condoms and spermicide – but my mom always claimed that our family had "good Catholic breeder genes" and I guess my body was trying to prove her right. His pregnancy went fine. I had some serious morning sickness for the first two trimesters, but that was the only drawback. Even labor and delivery was easier than I had expected. Remind me to tell you some time about how a custom built subwoofer played a role in my son's Christmas day arrival.

A couple years later when I was in graduate school and starting to lose myself again, I thought about surrogacy, or some other way to be pregnant but not have to deal with another actual child of my own. My husband Dwight and I decided to pursue that route, and we found a surrogacy agency to start the process. I matched with a same sex couple because at the time gay men were still facing significant challenges to building a family. I wanted these parts that I had to make a real difference if I was going to use them. The little girl who was the result of that surrogacy died of brain cancer at age 7, but I had a reprieve from the dysphoria and disassociation that I normally felt in my own skin for the nine months that I carried her.

Another couple of years went by, and I felt myself in need of some help again, so I did what had worked in the past, and started on another surrogacy. This second time around, I wanted more autonomy, so we went independent and matched with another same sex couple who were looking to find a traditional surrogate (where the surrogate and egg donor are the same person). We worked well together, and less than a year later there was an amazing little human who embodied her dads' desire to be dads.

Less than a month after surrogate daughter #2 was born, my sister died by her own hand. Really, she may have pulled the trigger, but her death was entirely because of her husband, a verbally and physically abusive jerk who preyed on women half his age. This wouldn't have necessarily been relevant, except that this added stress had me thinking about ways to deal with stress sooner than usual. Before a year was up, I was wanting (no, needing) a bit of decrease in my general anxiety levels. This sent my looking at surrogacy ads and forums, but the consensus at that point in time was that I was too old to begin another surrogacy journey. I could respect that, but it left me to figure out a newer (and ultimately healthier) way to deal with my dysphoria.

Finally, north of age 32, I found a term for what I was experiencing and how my body felt. Did I mention that I tend to be a little slow on the uptake? Around this same time, I was (finally) introduced to the term 'trans' and things started to fall into place. I discovered 'trans' and my world shifted.

I finally had the terms to use when I spoke. And those words finally felt right. I was a man. A guy. My father's son. My husband took the announcement in stride, saying that he wasn't horribly surprised and he knew that something had been going been brewing in my head. My own son, to whom I had given the prized name that belonged to my father, rolled with the punches beautifully. He's the one person who's never misgendered me through all this, and the fact that he's had to take flak at school is my one regret.

Coming out to my second surrogate daughter's dads was interesting to say the least, but one of them was a counselor in a university, and many of the students he saw were a part of the LGBTQ community. For them, though, they felt a definite loss. I initially came out to them as genderqueer, to test the waters a bit. My role in their life was very much a gendered role. Maybe I had been naïve, but I hadn't considered the close tie they had to me as "mama" until the end of the pregnancy and the birth of their little girl. In my own parenting, I was a parent first, and my husband and I frequently joked that he was more a mom than I was, changing diapers and washing laundry and such. It came as a surprise to me when my surrogate daughter's dads put so much emphasis on gender and insisted on calling me "mama" to their child. They took the announcement of my non-female gender well, and only slipped up on occasion.

After a few months of not losing my daughter's fathers, I broached the subject of trans-ness. When I came out to them, they had questions as to what brought about this new announcement. They were more upset that I thought they might not be accepting than any upset over this revelation. We eventually got past any hurt that there was, and have gone on to be the happy family that we were before- four dads and two kids, living in each other's' hearts and lives while separated by states.

Our little clan is not the typical one we all know, but we're happy, healthy, and the kids are all right. There aren't many others, but I know guys like me do exist, and I've met a couple of others. Western society assigns gender to nearly everything, and some of those assignations are simply asinine. The idea that nurturing children is a role for only half of the population, or that half of the population is somehow born with knowledge of how babies work – these are absurd at best and dangerous at worst.

Trying to fit people into neat, tidy boxes forces people to adapt to those boxes and change themselves to fit those boxes. The better, healthier, and more respectful option is to allow individuals to create their own space, and to declare themselves for all the world to know. I made do with what I had in the way of both knowledge and body parts. I've never fit either of the gender boxes that we've got in the US today very well. I've done what I could to make my own box, one that fits me, a trans man and a surrogate.

Maxfield Sparrow
Age – 50
Gendervague/Metagender/Epicene

16: Upon Realizing I am a Metagender Epicene
2017

I was assigned female at birth. As a toddler, I fought with my brother when he called me a girl. I assured him I was not a girl at all! I got a little older and learned more about bodies and came to accept that I must be a girl, no matter how I felt about it.

In adolescence, I read *The Marvelous Land of Oz* (Baum & Neill, 2000) and identified with the main character, Tippetarius, who was grudgingly transformed into the Empress Ozma at the end of the story. "I'm not a girl!" Tip protested, just as I had told my brother. But Oz needs the Empress and Tip must give up his identity. "I want to stay a boy [...] I don't want to be a girl!" Tip cried. Tip was spirited away; only Ozma remained.

I resented the ending of Baum's novel. Now, when I look back at the huge difference between how I felt about myself and my body at age 12 -- comfortable, flat-chested, not yet forced into gendered pigeonholes -- and the way

I felt about my body and my life at age 15 -- awkward, ashamed, and deformed -- I feel like I was forced to stop being Tippetarius, too. Unlike Ozma, I never grew to accept my new role.

Around that same time, a neighbor my age showed me a booklet that defined sex and gender as two separate things. She was confused and disgusted and sought my input. It was the first time I had seen the concepts teased apart. I finally had the language that allowed me to consider whether the identity that was written in my flesh was required to match the identity that was written in my spirit.

With the onset of puberty, I began to have a hard time even thinking or speaking of it as my body anymore. It became the body. In dreams I drove everywhere in a faulty vehicle with bad brakes and unresponsive steering. The body was simply my vehicle, the thing I had gotten stuck inside. The real me was invisible inside the illusion.

Separating sex and gender meant I could separate myself from the unwanted body that carried me through life. That distancing turned me into something of an accidental gnostic, discarding the body as unimportant and despised. I climbed inside my head and set up camp there, ignoring physicality. Things done to the body were not done to me. I was despondent in my apparent unknowability.

My identity was obscured by the idea that all women in

our culture hate their bodies thanks to impossible standards of beauty. Didn't hating the body merely prove my womanhood? Layered onto those thoughts were neurological traits of autism. I have alexithymia: I experience emotions but am unable to recognize them or name them. A lifetime of practice allows me to interpret my emotions from bodily sensations but I'm unable to recognize or regulate my emotions until they have grown overwhelmingly huge.

Additionally, I have a disconnect from physical embodiment. Some of that comes from a lifetime of trans denial but much of it comes from my divergent neurology. I have a hard time registering pain, illness, or even the space the body fills. I am dyspraxic -- I stumble and falter, struggling to maintain awareness of where and how the body is moving through space.

I cannot separate my gender identity from my autism. We Autistics have a word for that: gendervague. One definition of gendervague is "a gender identity that is highly influenced by being neurodivergent, and feels undefinable because of one's neurodivergence." Another definition is, "your gender is not definable with words because of one's status as neurodivergent" (strangeloved, n.d.). Obviously this essay would be over before it started if my only identity were gendervague. I can use words to discuss and define my gender, complicated and confusing though it is to me.

As a result of my autistic quirks, I didn't begin identifying as metagender until my 30s. Metagender means I don't feel like a woman and I don't feel like a man. I don't feel like a gender at all. But I don't feel "genderless," either. Metagender is a word that expresses feeling outside the entire paradigm of gender. I know, intellectually, that gender is a real thing. I know, compassionately, that people have genders and those genders are deeply felt and experienced. I spent a lot of time, starting with that pre-pubescent discovery of gender as something distinct from body, contemplating what my gender could be. I struggled to find it, to feel it, to know it. I felt like I had no gender. But the agender label seemed to say, "gender is. Some people have gender. I do not." Within myself, I still struggle to "see" gender. I have to take it on faith that gender is real. When it comes to myself, my faith in gender falters.

I am metagender because I just don't grasp gender at all. I accept it but I doubt I will ever really "get it" as some solid, visceral comprehension. That still left the vehicle my metagender spirit travels around in. I hated the chest. For years I tried, and failed, to get my doctor to sign off on a reduction. Secretly, I wanted more than a reduction. I sometimes, while "under the influence," mentioned that I wanted a body "streamlined, like a dolphin." Other times I'd refer to the furry, smooth sleekness of an otter. A couple of times, I asked, "wouldn't I look great with a beard?" People laughed when I said these things and I laughed along, letting myself down, hiding deeper inside my head, pretending my deepest dreams and desires were only a joke.

Being non-binary and metagender obscured my transmasculine leanings. As misery leaked from every pore,

I could only focus on trying to avoid making those around me miserable. My gendervague feelings and resulting metagender identity, combined with my pseudognostic alienation from all things body left me floundering in a free-floating, undefined, low-grade despair. I was so disconnected from the vehicle that I wasn't even sure why I was despairing.

It took me much longer to realize that I needed to change the somatic presentation of the vehicle. Being metagender had seemed like the last word. If I am not a man and not a woman, why care what vehicle I was riding around in? But I did care. Not realizing that I cared nearly killed me. Some of the distance I maintained from the body ... my body ... was due to my general neurology and overall makeup, but it turns out a lot of that disconnect was suppressed dysphoria leading me to separate from body to escape nearly unbearable pain and angst.

I was trying to understand myself better. I was trying to move past the overwhelming anxiety and depression that had dogged me my entire life. One day while sitting in meditation I connected the dots. I needed to change the vehicle. I needed to stop riding in the vehicle and take the wheel myself. I needed to reclaim the vehicle as a body. I needed to do whatever was necessary to own the body. I needed to change my hormonal foundation so I could own my body.

I endured a year of navel gazing and second-guessing myself after that realization. I was confused -- why go through something so huge and expensive and potentially dangerous as medical transition when I didn't feel gender? When I finally came to my "change or die" point a year later, I was forced to admit that I was suicidally depressed and that it was because I was so overflowing with dysphoria I could barely function.

And that's what led me to where I am today, four months into testosterone therapy and my only regret being that I didn't do this decades sooner. I know I wasn't ready yet back then. Still, I wish I could have figured things out earlier or have been born and raised in a time and place less invested in thwarting the kind of self-understanding I needed. I'm not a woman. I'm not a man. But I need a flat chest and a deeper voice to feel more comfortable in this body.

When I first came out as metagender, I asked people to use the singular they for my pronouns. No one remembered and I was frequently called "she," the pronoun set I am the least comfortable with. I went a step further and asked people to stop using any pronouns at all. If you need to refer to me, I said, use my name. My name is my pronoun. That was easier for others than singular they, although I still got called "she" too much and it really grated on me with a pain my alexithymia can only interpret as physically wrenching.

When I decided I was going to medically transition to a masculine presentation, I asked people to call me "he" and, for the most part, they have. I will feel ready for more ambiguity again, I am certain, once I have progressed far enough in my medical transition that strangers call me "sir" and "he." People will be just as wrong assuming I am a man as they have been assuming I was a woman. But, for reasons I can't adequately communicate (and might choose to blame on being gendervague), I am much more comfortable misgendered as a man than I ever was with it being assumed I was a woman.

I use the word transgender because I am not cis. But I also use the word transsexual -- which is not a word one should casually apply to others, only to one's self. Many trans people are offended by the word "transsexual," viewing it as too clinical and emblematic of an oppressive gatekeeper approach to trans issues. I embrace the word because it so clearly describes what is happening in my life right now. I am changing every day and it is not my gender that is changing. My gender, such as it is, remains the same. It is my body -- my sex -- that I am changing. I embrace the term "sex change" because that is what I am doing. I am changing my sex, my body, so that it is comfortable for me to live inside. I am having a sex change because I needed to change my body in order to feel at home inside it. I have a visceral need to be seen and treated as a person on the masculine side of a sliding scale of gender expression.

While I talk about being FTM (female to male) because that is how I can find the people and resources I need for this journey, I actually identify as FTE -- female to epicene. When I see my true body, I am streamlined and I have no external genitalia spoiling that contour. My metagender spirit needed an epicene body in which to dwell.

Epicene is a term from linguistics, referring to those words -- like cousin or doctor -- applied to male and female alike but with no intrinsic gender. And that is how I think of this body now. It is not a female body or a male body. It is evolving toward traits pertaining to both, but it's neither. My body is an epicene body housing a metagender person.

Some people may see my intentionally masculinized body and believe it is simply male, just as some fans were vehemently against the announcement that the 13th Doctor on *Doctor Who* is wearing a female-presenting body. "Doctor" is an epicene word like my body is an epicene body. "Doctor" has no inherent sex or gender to it; it could be both. Or neither. Like me.

This arduous journey has been worth every struggle. I still have far to go, but now I catch a glimpse: I have taken the wheel and am steering my body home.

17: The In-between
2017

I didn't know that I was transgender until I was 20 years old. When I was little, as young as 2 or 3, I had no concept of gender other than the word boy described those with "outies" and girl described those with "innies". My parents were never strict about gender roles. I have a little sister about the same age and a sister 12 years older. All three of us were allowed to do, wear, or like anything regardless of what was deemed feminine or masculine. I did happen to enjoy things that were usually enjoyed by boys rather than girls, and everyone always commented on what a "tomboy" I was. I was often mistaken as a boy, and my dad always said, "come on, son" when we set off to some adventure little boys often go on with their fathers. Throughout elementary school, most of my friends were boys, including my best friend who lived next door, and we played like brothers. Even up through high school my guy friends always exclaimed that I was so cool because I was just like a guy in a girl's body. They had no idea how right they were.

When I was 19, and already married for a year, I moved to New York City. At this point, I had only recently heard of the term transgender and was only vaguely aware that people "like that" existed. But for some reason the topic fascinated me when I learned of it. My first job in New York was as a canvasser raising money for the Human Rights Campaign, a notable LGBT advocate. Many of my coworkers were members of the queer community in some capacity or another. I had two coworkers who are trans women. I also met someone on the job who was non-binary, my first time hearing such a concept articulated.

This look into gender that I didn't know was possible immediately started a process of cognitive and physical dissonance within myself, which I later learned was called dysphoria. I was married to a straight man, and our relationship meant the world to me – easily the most important thing in my life. "Now I know that there are people out there who don't just feel more like the gender they weren't assigned at birth, but they really are guys instead of girls. But I couldn't be one of them, right? That's such a rare phenomenon and it couldn't happen to me. I must be making this up."

I struggled for weeks, falling deeper into depression as the dysphoria wore me down. I was so sure that even if I was transgender, as I was nearly accepting of at this point, I could never do anything about it. It would ruin my life for certain. Eventually, I couldn't keep my struggle hidden from my husband any longer. I'd hinted a bit for years, even before I knew the concept of trans-ness existed, that I felt more male than female. I sobbed and told him I think I'm transgender and I need to transition. I explained that I don't feel like a man, exactly, but I don't feel like a woman at all. The very thought of me as a woman is wrong and foreign and I have no idea what being a woman feels like, because I have never been one. I didn't know what that made me, but I knew I was not a "she" and it hurt me to be called that. I wanted it to stop.

To his eternal credit, he held me and told me it didn't matter, and that he would support me no matter what. That it might change our relationship, but that he would always be behind me. And from that point on, he stopped calling me "she", "her", and "wife", and I became "his person." I decided to start taking Testosterone and I changed my legal gender marker. I already have an androgynous birth name, so luckily, I could keep that with no negative feelings. I came out at work as FtM because I felt too embarrassed to admit I am non-binary. The absent gender identity I felt as a small child, the one that was driven away by commands to put on a shirt and sit like a lady, had returned, and I the only gendered term I felt fully at ease with was "guy". Not a man or a boy, and not sir, but a guy, whatever that means.

Now, a year and a half into my transition, few know (and fewer remember) that I am not, in fact, male. I now know that the most accurate description for my gender might sound something like "genderfluid, ranging from agender to demi-male". Sometimes I feel like I have no gender at all, while other times I feel decidedly more male than anything, but never entirely a man. Man is not what I am, and that's fine. However, my gender is seen as invalid most of the time, and disgusting in far too many cases. It is believed to be made up to quell a generation of attention-seeking babies who thrive on victimhood. A few see it as a danger to society. In the best-case scenarios in my own day to day experience, it is simply forgotten because I look, sound, and act like a typical cis-male, and so that is how I am perceived. I pass as cis 100% of the time, and have for several months.

I am one of the lucky ones in that masculine pronouns don't cause any dysphoria. I love hearing them and fully identify with them. But I do feel sad over the erasure of my gender identity at times. Mostly because of the harm it does to those who do feel just as much dysphoria over being identified as male as they do being identified as female. I know people in that situation, and the struggle I was feeling at the beginning of my transition is a daily reality for them and may be for the rest of their lives. I have been personally stunned and am immensely grateful that I, and transgender individuals as a whole, are being accepted by many and the support for our community is growing as the years go by. I thought I would be faced with discrimination in my small, republican town full of churches. Instead, I am treated like any other young man in town, including by those who devoutly practice a religion that I had thought declared me an undesirable.

Now, what I hope for is that non-binary humans will be accepted into the transgender community and recognized as equally real and valid as binary transgender men and women. Gender is a wibbly-wobbly mess of biology mixed with man-made concepts, animal instincts and intellectual progress. The more I learn about gender and physical sex, the more I understand that it is not and has never been as cut and dry as 2 boxes where everyone should fit, and a garbage can for the factory defects. It is a complex web of amino acids, neurology, single alleles on certain chromosomes, environmental changes in the womb, environmental situations in early childhood, and a thousand other variables you could throw into the mix.

In my worldview, one highly influenced by scientific minds like Carl Sagan, Neil DeGrasse Tyson, and Richard Dawkins, humans are a single species among the 8.7 million others on this planet. Sex and gender in the rest of nature are nowhere close to being limited to 2 options that always like up in neat combinations. It's a big biological mess, and we are no different.

18: Changes
2017

I was in Houston, 2016. Two and a half weeks after Orlando, I was working with the Red Cross in the area to help survivors of floods that had wrecked homes, cars, and belongings. We grabbed lunch at a cheap restaurant, and before we left, I ducked into the bathroom.

I was in a stall when I heard the door slam open. It seems impossibly loud to me now, but things change in memories.

"HEY", came the thundering voice. "IS THERE A MAN IN HERE?"

Well, there certainly is now, I thought to myself, sitting there on the toilet seat in a stall in a little bathroom marked "WOMEN" in the middle of Texas.

It's easy to pretend that I started yelling back, that I educated a new person about the gender binary.

The woman in the stall next to me didn't say anything. Looking back now, it seems obvious why. Sometimes questions come up that have nothing to do with you, and you wait for their intended target to answer them instead.

I deliberately pitched my voice high, "Uh, no?"

He muttered and shuffled but didn't blow my stall down, and eventually he left.

The entire exchange had taken less than a minute. My new coworkers had no idea what had happened, and I wasn't about to tell them.

Two and a half weeks ago, my mom had asked me what my new name was for the first time. My sister had asked me what pronouns I wanted. Two and a half weeks ago, I was curled up on the floor of a hotel bathroom thinking about dying, because it seemed easier than having to deal with the constant tragedies of having to reinvent myself, of having to decide whether or not to tell my parents that I was agender and queer and that I hated the name that they'd given me.

How long is long enough to wait? When does it stop being a "phase" and start being a life?

I got my first big haircut when I was ten or twelve. My mom did it. It feels almost ceremonial now: tying my hair into a long braid, cutting it off, and saving it in a box. It felt exciting back then. Not for gender reasons, I think, but just because it was a new thing, and new things are exciting when you're younger. Hair was less about gender and more about confidence. When you have long hair, you can hide behind it. If you're nervous, you can chew on it.

I wouldn't say I was a nervous child, but I liked being able to hide behind my hair, and cutting it felt like a new way to say that I wasn't afraid.

The longest I grew it out was to my shoulder blades: and due to quirks of anatomy, even then strangers called me "sir". I was tall, and had mostly given up dresses, and usually I went with it, because I thought it was funny. I was sixteen.

"It doesn't matter to me," I remember telling my dad, after a salesperson had asked us gentlemen what she could do for us today, and his response had included the word "daughter", loud in the store.

"I think it does." was his response. "I think it does more than you think."

...Well, dad, I guess it's possible for both of us to be wrong.

I think the last time I wore a skirt was at a wedding. I don't remember whose wedding, or even which state we were in, but I remember that the skirt was knee length and dark grey and paisley. I remember hating it, I remember trying to go back in the house and change, that this was a mistake. But we didn't have time, and so we left in my dark paisley skirt that I had loved so much when I had found it at goodwill.

Sometimes, people change. My mom pointed out once that as a younger me, I had loved dresses and skirts, as if to say that because of this one fact, nothing else mattered now.

I remember looking in the mirror at age ten, seeing my chest and knowing that I would never be able to run around without a shirt on again, and hating it. I remember lying motionless on my front in Idaho, feeling trapped and horrified by my own body's wrongness. I remember putting on a binder for the first time and having to weigh the pros and cons of sleeping in it:

Pros: I go to sleep feeling *right*, I wake up feeling *right*

Cons: I break a rib and die in my sleep, long term rib damage, bruises, back pain, headaches from not enough oxygen

It was almost an even vote.

I changed my name more than three months ago, and there are still things I need to figure out. I got my name changed on my library card just last week: at the library's Trans Pride booth. My parents changed my name on their insurance, and just last week my dad sent me a text:

"You would be proud, today mom and I schooled a lawyer on A-gender.. I think the lawyer was impressed. She said she thinks it's cool a person has the ability to do this. Be proud, we are trying one lawyer at a time

Love you :D"

I guess it's possible for both of us to be wrong. But I also guess it's possible for both of us to be right. Sometimes, people change.

Sam Lacovara
Age – 23
Non-Binary

19: Gender as Affect
"Feeling" the Radical Potential for Queer Survival Beyond Binaries
2016

> "Gender is the poetry each of us makes out of the language we are taught." - Leslie Feinberg, *Trans Liberation: Beyond Pink or Blue*

For me, the journey to identify as neither a man nor a woman was as follows: compulsory heterosexuality and cisgenderism groomed me to be a cis, straight woman. As I entered adolescence, I began identifying as a cisgender queer woman, acknowledging that I was *definitely* not straight. I started to question gender in college and claimed a genderfluid identity, but still within the binary of man and woman, feeling like my identity moved between those two genders. After more exposure to the vastness of transgender identities, I claimed a non-binary label, and then, in attempts to intentionally challenge the gender binary more directly, discovered and named what I call my "affective genders."

Our understanding of normative binary genders has been constructed mainly through colonialism, specifically the raced, gendered, and classed expectations that colonialism has attached to performances of masculinity and femininity. In order to separate our understandings of gender from these oppressive, racist, and imperialist cultural implications, we must resist, and eventually transcend, binary gender by decolonizing our own genders. When I say decolonize our genders, I mean intentionally challenge the ideas and requirements that colonialism has placed upon our identities and performances of them.

Gendered experiences are informed by one's race, class, ability, and other intersecting identities. An experience is never just what is happening at the given moment, it is directly related to everything that has come before it, personally and historically. While we may have all been taught to reproduce the colonialist gender binary, our relationships to and histories with it are very different, as are our modes of reproduction. This coming to consciousness of affective gender is reliant on one's access to the resources necessary to unlearn compulsory heterosexuality and cisgenderism.

My ability to comprehend and re-negotiate my own identity was one of privilege and opportunity. I have been fortunate to have radical queer activist communities and academic spaces where theorizing gender was accessible to, encouraged and required of me. Therefore, it is of the utmost importance that I recognize and acknowledge the privilege I have as a young, college-educated, trans-masculine white person. It is because of those specific intersections that I am able to do this theorizing, as I am given the space and resources to do it without constant threats of physical violence that are unavoidably present in the daily lives of gender-nonconforming folks of color. However, affective gender has the potential to affirm the experiences of those identities that exist and intersect in multiple, and perhaps conflicting, spheres. Affective gender is constructed completely by the self, and therefore is able to do whatever kind of work an individual needs it to, and can be expressed in the ways that are most comfortable to and safe for that person.

I argue that masculinity and femininity are expressions completely unrelated to gender identity, and separating these performances from our identities is the first step in decolonizing and destabilizing the binary. Realistically, all expressions of masculinity and femininity exist on a spectrum between the two poles, some just more distinctly (and intentionally) fluid than others. This could manifest in ways as simple as a cis woman wearing her hair short, or a cis man acting as the primary caretaker of children rather than breadwinner.

Audre Lorde, feminist scholar and poet, described the erotic as an untapped power within each of us, "between the beginnings of our sense of self and the chaos of our strongest feelings" (1984: 56). For me this

151

eroticism, one that is completely separate from the physical or the sexual, lives deep in my belly, and is awoken by specific sensory stimuli. I propose we construct gender as affect, based in our most personal experiences; we must acknowledge the things that make us *feel*. Affective gender doesn't require a specific set of pronouns, nor does it require that pronouns "match" a body or expression. Built from feelings, affective genders are limitless and inherently without rules.

The intense emotions we feel daily, and our relationship to their causes, are integral to our identities. A more comprehensive definition of affective gender would be one's emotional, mental, spiritual, physical, and/or otherwise psycho-, socio-, and physiological connections to oneself, one's environment, and others. Put simply, it is sense of internal and external presence and connection.

I've named my primary affective gender "banjender," after the eroticism that listening to the sound of a banjo makes me feel. It is a quick, folky, and plunky gender. It can be muffled, acoustic, tinny or steeley, bright or twangy. Even in its most intense forms, banjender is a relatively soft, mellow gender. I say "primary affective gender" because there are various experiences that awaken my erotic, and my affective gender identities are fluid and multiple so as to acknowledge and prioritize each of those emotional responses as they occur. Other affective genders of mine include the scent of fresh brewed coffee; the sight of the moon and constellations in a clear night's sky; and the combination of October leaves crunching under heavy boots, chilly winds gently stinging flushed cheeks, and the warm, distant scent of fire. Each of these sensations causes an equally powerful and emotional experience for me that is much more foundationally linked to my personhood than my expressions of masculinity and femininity; therefore, I name my gender(s) after them.

Lorde calls attention to the phrase "it feels right to me" as the ultimate form of knowledge and guidance (1984: 56). Affective gender is the thing that feels right to you. It is a mode of naming and understanding that acknowledges one's place in, and relationship to, a given moment. Affective gender is not to be conflated with the experience of *really* enjoying something. That said, I do not simply enjoy the sound of a banjo the way many others do, my emotional response to it is so intensely related to my sense of self that I *am* banjender.

Affective gender is the emotion one feels in response to a physical event; it is not something that *actually* happens in a way that can be tangibly experienced by anyone but the self. Even in a room full of people listening to the same music, no one but I can feel *my* specific eroticism that is associated with the music of a banjo. Because that feeling occurs within myself alone, it is my truth and no one else's. This is the trickiness that comes with any truth claim: if it is not universally true, can it be considered true at all? Does authenticity come from mass validation, or the insistence (even if only by one person) that a truth exists? My truth claim that I *am* banjender enables me to find comfort in my non-binary identity, knowing that regardless of the pronouns someone misuses for me, or the binary gender expectations projected onto me, my queer consciousness can survive within my affective gender.

In her discussion of affective solidarity, Clare Hemmings argued "that moment of affect... is the core of transformation" and that it is "an unstable entity and its impact cannot be controlled" (2012: 157). That moment of uncontrollable affect (for me, hearing the banjo and feeling erotic), followed by the conscious recognition of its happening, is the inception of the infinite possibility of affective gender. This coming to consciousness would allow all individuals to have their own affective genders, limitless in terms of quantity and content. However, this process is inextricably tied to one's involvement in queer community and exposure to non-binary identities.

The language that we are given to define our gender identities and expressions, even as it becomes broader, still relies on binarist connotations. Words like transwoman and tomboy, while they express deviance from normative gender identity and expression, still rely on the roots of the gender binary (man/woman, boy/girl) for context. This additive model of reforming language clearly does not do enough to expand (nor ideally break) the boundaries of gender.

Instead of a designated list of specific words that are acceptable to use in describing one's gender identity, I argue that any and *every* word should, and must, be available for naming one's affective gender. Leslie Feinberg said, "we didn't choose these words. They don't fit all of us. It's hard to fight an oppression without a name connoting pride, a language that honors us" (1998: 206). That is exactly what I am arguing we change. Just as I can use the word banjo in my gender identity, any other word can be similarly co-opted and incorporated. The radical possibilities of affective gender are contingent on the ability to choose our own words, to make language honor our identities.

Whether you can identify an affective gender for yourself or not, the very concept is liberating for everyone. As Feinberg said, "trans liberation has meaning for you-no matter how you define or express your sex or gender" (1998: 5). The ability to access one's eroticism opens up endless possibilities for community-building, as the strongest communities are built not through shared identity, but shared experience. This is not unlike Hemmings' concept of affective solidarity, which, rather than grounding communities in shared identity, instead "is proposed as a way of focusing on modes of engagement that start from the affective dissonance that feminist politics necessarily begins from" (2012: 148). Her project seeks to move from affective dissonance, and modes of individual experience, to affective solidarity and collective work, which is precisely what I aim to do in moving from transgender and non-binary identity to affective gender.

Lorde stated that "in order to be utilized, our erotic feelings must be recognized. The need for sharing deep feeling is a human need" (1984: 58). In sharing my affective gender through this essay, I have vulnerably opened myself up to the possibility of mocking and critique, but also the possibility of power building and validation. The latter two are simultaneously self-serving and selfless; I can have my own identity affirmed while guiding others on how to experience their full erotic potential. That potential is, to quote Lorde, "an internal sense of satisfaction to which, once we have experienced it, we know we can aspire. For having experienced the fullness of this depth of feeling and recognizing its power, in honor and self-respect we can require no less of ourselves" (1984: 54). These experiences of significant affect are happening to all of us daily, whether we are conscious of them or not. To deprive them of their potential to serve our eroticism is a disservice to our queerness, our communities, our marginalized intersections, our futures, and our very senses of self.

There is an undeniable utopianism to affective gender identity, and it lends itself to critique of individualism, and questions of the logistics of community building. *How could these identities be considered legitimate? What would come of the binary gender categories? Where would social boundaries start and end?* However, I find this puzzling utopianism to be useful, important, and productive. As José Esteban Muñoz (1999), also a defender of the utopian, argued, "although utopianism has become the bad object of much contemporary political thinking, we nonetheless need to hold on to and even *risk* utopianism if we are going to engage in the labor of making a queerworld" (p. 25).

That's what I'm asking you do. I'm asking you to risk all that you have been taught, all that you know about gender identity and expression. I'm asking you to dig down, deep into your belly, and find what feels *right*, then name yourself after that feeling. I'm asking you to engage in this labor, and build a utopian, affective, erotic queerworld with me.

20: Middle Ground
2017

It is 1989 and I am still an only child, with a future little sister just months away. It is on the cusp of summer and I have just turned four years old. I have a mop of white-blonde curly hair, freckles dot my cheeks and nose and I run around like I have free reign of our old house and big yard. When I am left to my own devices, I make my own fun, getting wrapped up in an imaginary world where the trees can talk and practicing my kicks, in my red and blue karate costume. And I am absolutely obsessed with the Teenage Mutant Ninja Turtles and every cent I get given goes into saving for another figurine for my collection.

As the days grow warmer and longer, one of my earliest and most vivid childhood memories unfolds. I am out on the balcony with my father, in the warmth of the afternoon sun and he, the master storyteller, begins telling me about the plant he is tending to. It looks like it is getting ready to flower and he says that it is no ordinary plant, but one that only flowers once every ten years. The pollen that the flower contains has magical powers and will allow us to be whatever we want for a day.

This story spans days or maybe even weeks, and then as the anticipation grows, my father asks me what I want to be for a day. I tell him I wanted to fly. But that is a lie and that lie is the reason I remember this all so vividly. Flying would have been exhilarating but what would have been even better, was to be a boy for a day. But little four-year-old me somehow knows that this is too big a thing to say.

Conveniently, my mother leaves the plant out on the balcony on a particularly hot day, mere weeks before its mystical bloom and the plant is burnt to a crisp. The plant may be dead, but my secret wish isn't. I try to be more like a boy, doing what boys do. I go to the toilet and instead of sitting down, I remain standing and awkwardly try to take aim. It doesn't go well, and I end up with pee trickling down my leg and drops all over the toilet seat. I try my best to clean it up, in my four-year-old way but of course my mother catches on. She asks me what I am doing and I mumble an embarrassed something and never try to pee like a boy again.

This all remains etched into my little brain, along with a lot of angst, guilt and confusion. These feelings follow me through the rest of my childhood, which is filled with prince and super hero scenarios and summer holidays spent without a shirt.

-

It is 2000, we all survived the Y2K, but I am barely surviving the hell pit of utter misery that is puberty and catholic high school as a closet case. All the fourteen-year-old girls around me, proudly show off their budding breasts with new push-up bras, while I hunch my shoulders forward as far as they will go, hating that my body is betraying me by turning me into a woman. I hate what is happening to me – the boobs, the widening hips, my period and the crushes I have on girls, that I spend so much energy trying to deny. I have a seething hate for myself, but I write bad poetry, play a lot of sport and keep my grades up and no one seems to notice and I manage to survive.

-

It is 2007 and I have just clawed most of my way out of the depths of something deeper and darker than your regular teenage angst. With my twenty first birthday behind me, I finally summon the courage and come out to my mother by way of three little words scrawled on a tear-stained post-it note. "I am gay" it reads, in my nervous cursive, unlocking me from my closet and allowing me space to dress like a teenage skater boy, walk with a little more swagger and more openly show interest in girls.

For a little while it all seems to make sense and I throw myself into this new life I have finally allowed myself to live. I make some gay friends and we go out every weekend to the same gay bar and see the same gay girls and it all feels new and exciting. For the first time for as long as I can remember, I don't feel fear, because those three words allow me space to explore a truer side of myself.

It is 2017 and my entire twenties have flashed me by and I feel like I don't have much to show for it, besides a dozen stamps in my passport and a hefty university loan. It has taken me almost exactly ten years since I stepped out of the closet to get to the place I am right now, just back from a yoga class and settling in to an evening of reading and writing, propped up in the bed I share each night with my gorgeous girlfriend.

Over these past ten years my relationship with those three words I wrote on that post-it, has taken various turns. There were moments when I revelled in my gay or lesbian identity, so proud of myself and my community. And then there were the couple of years, where shame started to encroach, and I went through an awkward semi-heterosexual phase, complete with asshole boyfriend and a wardrobe of now long-abandoned maxiskirts. That was all part of growing up, of working it out, I guess.

And so that brings me back to now, reflecting and writing and waiting for my girlfriend to get home from a late bar shift. I am trying to make sense of a lifetime of barely articulated thoughts, the kind that linger on the outskirts and never make it in to full blown consciousness. I know that even when they haven't been in full view, the thoughts have always been there. I have spent thirty-two years trying to work out what these feelings are and what I am and still don't have an answer. All I can say with any certainty, is that gender is a total head fuck.

At twenty-one, it was such a massive deal for me to pull

myself out of my messed up, terrifying head space and come out as gay, or a lesbian, or a lady-lover. These identities allow me to be truer to myself. They allow me to love women and provide some flexibility in the way I walk and talk in the world. It has taken me ten years, however, to realise that these identities are not enough, that they fail to grasp at something that has nothing to do with who I love; my gendered self. I'm still failing and flailing when it comes to finding the right words to capture something of the gender territory in which I exist. It is like I have been tongue-tied my entire life.

I don't know how to articulate this eloquently, so I will tell you some things about me... I honestly think I would have been happier and life would have made more sense had I been a boy and then a man. My body had other plans though and it betrayed me by becoming all woman-like, with boobs and blood. But despite living in this female skin for quite some time now, I just can't wrap my head around what it might feel like to be happily, comfortably woman.

I like to play around, trying to get my body to mould into something closer to what I feel would be more right. Sometimes I lay on my back without a bra, so gravity does its job and I can lift my head and gaze down at myself and feel the thrill of seeing a flat chest. I get that same thrill, every time I see glimpses of androgyny in my reflection. I cut my hair off a year ago and threw out my maxiskirts three years ago. I have a delightful collection of high-tops, that are probably too young for me, but they make me feel like I am reclaiming some of the boyhood I never really had.

I am girlfriend to my partner but there are moments when I feel the boundaries blur, when I am something closer to a man, wrapping her in my arms. I look at transmen on YouTube and Instagram with intense, addictive curiosity. But something holds me back from going there. I want the flat chest, but I don't want the surgery. I want the more muscular build from testosterone shots but not the pimples from a second puberty nor the clit dick. I want to change out of this female skin, but into what, I don't know. I just know the face staring back at me in the mirror each morning, is not fully recognisable, like in my half sleepy state, I was expecting something different. I was hoping for beautiful androgyny or better still a full remodel, a redo or a parallel reality in which I am man not middle ground.

I tell myself I am not supposed to believe in a gender binary, that I don't want to go from one box to another. The middle ground should be okay. This deliciously queer, undefinable, undeniable space should be okay. Whatever and wherever this middle ground is, I'm still adjusting, still finding my place, still deciding if this is actually okay.

Sé Sullivan
Age – 55
Genderfluid Queer

21: It Gets Different Not Better

2017

Trans Remembrance Day 2017...

The effects of non-conforming Gender, abandonment, psychological violence, and sexual abuse still impact my life daily. As an adult, I struggle with depression, self-care, and have considered suicide over the years, including during this research project. I have been at the forefront of what we could call the modern Queer, Trans movement, a movement like many that started in the 1960s and owes a great deal of its momentum to the global independent movements rejecting imperialism: The Black Panthers, Brown Berets, and yes, the Black Trans, Queer and Cis Feminists who continue to lead the way. I have and had a front-row seat to this history/moment because I was an out Queer child when I was taken hostage by those wanting the replication of a white heter-onormative child to grow up and reproduce more little, white, straight kids.

When I refused to be hailed (Althusser 1971) by the Gender apparatus (Repo 2016), when I refused to acknowledge the assumptions of the colonized mind (Fanon 1967), when I liked the character Vera/Vicente in the film The Skin I Live In (Almodóvar 2011), when I named myself outside of the flesh that is visible, the flesh that others name, when I refused that hailing as an aberrant or a deviant or a Frankenstein (Stryker 1994), and I take on the deviant, aberrant, or deviant as a floating identity marker and rob you of your intended violence, I secure my own hailing for a brief moment, and in those names I turned around, and for a fleeting temporal moment, my flesh is home. So, the effects are still happening every day, whether I have to go to the bathroom, or I am being pulled over by TSA at the airport, or by customs while crossing false borders to present on gender fluidity and the violence that accompanies it.

When I am in the grocery store, when I am hanging out with my friends, I get mis-gendered every day. I can pass for a white straight or queer dude, a hard Butch, or the fetishizing of my body that places it outside the constraints of Gender and sex expectation. The freak, the experiment, the person who is afraid to be seen as queer and seeks you out because you can pass for what they need, and the shame I feel when that touch has been the only comfort I could find, to offer my flesh on the down-low, fetishizing my own flesh for touch.

The wanting of touch, the need for companionship; I, like everyone else, crave companionship, be that monogamous or polygamous. I get misgendered in the classroom, the bar room, the protest rally, with or without facial hair. Not being seen: that's been the issue the whole time. I have been socialized as a woman with which I have a complicated history and relationship. Some people think, because of my masculinity, I was socialized to be masculine. Men of all ethnic persuasions, once they realize that I am not a cisgendered heteronormative man, often get very aggressive and violent with me.

Actually, I have lived on the fringes, having had my socializing on the parameters of the edges of both. I never fit in with the girls; I never fit in with the boys, so there it is, the space of the third-gendered. I am always, and have always been, on the edges of the assumptions placed on me. This is what I feel is the core issue for anyone who transgresses Gender: ours is a crime of deception. The crime of deception is that you (the general you) made an assumption, and when I correct you, your embarrassment, judgment, or trans/queer phobia rushes over you, and violence becomes the response. The deception is that you were attracted to me, that we were having a man-to-man conversation, that your wife/girlfriend thought I was desirable, that you thought I was desirable. Deception and desirability are at the root of the lie that the Gender apparatus builds as a cornerstone of oppression.

As a Queer butch and/or a fluid masculine person, I always had occupations like construction, or security, or the door at bars. These were the options in the 1980s, as mainstream companies did not hire Queers, especially masculine ones. So, is my rough exterior of my own making, or has it been shaped by the availability of the sociopolitical climate? Yes. Gender is a bio-political construction of the temporal and material conditions of the times in which it lives.

I, too, learned white patriarchal masculinity was a double edge sword, it was an identity that represents oppression and is the same location that makes my desirability complex. When I lecture today, I start the conversation with the question, "How do we get comfortable with being uncomfortable?" I know that looking like a white masculine person is a privilege and that my queerness mitigates that privilege. I stand on the edge, teetering between, again in the third space, not one or the other, but always knowing that the Gender violence I experience is also informed and structured by racism. I guess what I trying to get to is this: the fight continues and I remain here, trying to be part of the solution (Sullivan 2017).

Shalen Lowell
Age – 25
Agender and Genderfluid

22: Exclusion Everywhere:
Surmounting Forced Binarization to Identify as Agender
2017

I have the eyes of strangers trained on me everywhere: in the bathroom (either gendered bathroom), at work, when writing in the bookstore on Saturday mornings, at dinner with my boyfriend, at family parties—both strangers and distant relatives alike attempting to read me, to "clock" me, to gender me—in essence, to figure out *what* I am. "Is that a guy or a girl?" "That person has breasts, but they don't quite match with the body." "What kind of genitals do they have?" I see these questions flashing across their eyes, in their lingering stares. Those gawking stares are hurtful: they delegitimize me; they make me feel like an outlaw and anomaly in my own body. I feel like I'm breaking some set of unspoken societal rules by being nonbinary. No matter how comfortable I feel in any of my genders (including agender), I'll always be an outcast. Even the act of wearing my "Gender Roles are Dead," "Genderfluid," or "This Is What Trans Looks Like" shirts is rebellious: on the off-chance a transphobe or bigot glimpses it, I feel I'll be reported to the state or the police or some other such authority for being a gender "variant." These are the thoughts, worries, and concerns that—in an undercurrent—plague me, and consume almost every of my waking moments.

Despite these negative societal pressures, I've found considerable comfort outside the gender binary, both in terms of presentation and identity. For years I waged a hard-fought battle against my nonbinary-ness, which is evident in the spectrum of genders with which I identified, and from which, ultimately, I moved on, as I found more suitable identities for my true self. I went from identifying as "female" (though the terms "girl," "lady," "miss," "female," and the alike never quite fit me); to identifying as a demigirl; to anything but female; to wanting to ID as a "guy"; to wanting to ID as a transguy; to finding no comfort in any of those labels until I claimed genderqueer; and then genderfluid; and, finally, I settled on genderfluid and agender. My pronouns have gone through a similar shift: I went from using "she" all the time, to feeling wary about hearing "she," to experimenting with "they" with a few close friends, to using "they" all the time in my closest social circles, to introducing myself as "they" as I meet anyone new, to using "they" all the time except with my extended family. That's not to say that anyone who identifies along the nonbinary spectrum, or outside the gender binary at all, must use the pronoun "they." This is my personal pronoun transition.

Within my genderfluidity, I identify as multiple nonbinary identities: agender, nonbinary trans in general, sometimes nonbinary "guy," and just nonbinary, without any qualifiers. Ironically, I draw the most strength and satisfaction from identifying as agender and nonbinary genderfluid; there's less gender confusion for me outside the binary (ironic in the sense that people, even MOGAI and LGBTQ people, can be confused and, in some instances, more skeptical and less accepting of nonbinary identities). As nonbinary, I have less gender dysphoria. At the risk of sounding cliché, nonbinary just "clicks." Being nonbinary feels right with who I am.

I "came out" as agender *years* after graduating college, so I side-stepped the social exclusion, prejudice, and fallout that experience may well have entailed at any higher education Catholic, conservative institution. However, as the time passes and my comfort in my agender identity strengthens, it's becoming increasingly clear that I'm going to have to come out at work—and invite those worries within such a process I thought I'd side-stepped. I assumed I would, in the next year or so, move onto another job and start fresh, coming out there, but it looks like I'll be at this job for a while. As is, between work and my personal life, I feel I'm a living duality. Every time I hear the pronoun "she" when I'm being addressed or referred to, it's like a "ping" against my ear. I could muffle the sound and ignore it before, but it's ringing way too clear these days for me to do so. Moreover, I have this awkward, uncomfortable, dynamic where I'm friends with a good portion of my coworkers (with whom I hang out outside work), and I've *sort of* come out to *some* of them. But what happens with pronouns? Do I fully come out and insist on them using "they," but say "she" is okay for when we're at work? It's a delicate line to toe.

Is it asking too much of them to use two pronouns, switching between the work/personal environments? Is it too confusing? Do I risk losing any conservative friends I may have, to insist on pronoun correction? These questions and many more, I must consider.

As an agender individual, and one who's genderfluid identity consists of *multiple* nonbinary identities, I feel just as excluded from binary transgender spaces as I do from binary cisheteronormative spaces. Even in supposedly safe spaces for genderfluid and agender individuals, the gender binary is still upheld as an ideal: I often see countless genderfluid individuals posting two opposing pictures on the Facebook groups of which I am a member, one being their "female" presentation, and one being their "male" presentation. I am by no means mocking any of these individuals; every person has the right to live out and present their gender(s) as they choose, and to express their authentic self. This is also not to discredit those among my community who are bigender, and either present in the binary or identify as such. This is merely an example that, even in spaces wherein gender and presentation is fluid and all genders are to be respected, binary gender presentation is still upheld. I'm genderfluid, one of those identities being agender, and I feel excluded because I always present myself outside the binary: as "femme" and "masculine," and neither and both all at once. To me, I don't "look" like any gender, which is exactly how I want to live my life.

Despite my comfort, eschewing the binary came with unintended consequences for me, one of which I was not fully aware until I dipped my toe—or perhaps forcibly waded into—the dating pool post-undergraduate college. Dating as nonbinary was rough. That's the nicest remark I can make about the situation. Dating in your mid-20s is confusing, frustrating, and fraught with letdowns as is, never mind trying to navigate your identity during the process. I'm no longer female-identified, but I don't "pass" enough for most people, queer or not, to accept me as a "guy," further complicating dating with even queer cisgender people. I went on a few dates with a couple of cis women who identified as queer, but even dating within the LGBTQ community, I still felt uncomfortable. I'm bisexual, so attraction wasn't the issue on my part. My gender was the inhibitor. I hadn't been outright told my gender or gender presentation was the reason someone didn't want to date me, not in so many words at least. But that reality was intimated a number of times. I still get my period; I even pack "down there" on occasion. I rarely shave my legs or armpits, and wear almost every type of clothing under the sun (except for heels)—and, to many, I express my body and agenderness in a very "masculine way." If you identify as nonbinary, however you dress is nonbinary. But where the dating pool is concerned, because of how I specifically identify and dress, I felt I carved out an expression for myself to which little (especially cisgender) people were attracted to.

Only when I met my boyfriend, Shea, did I realize how amazing dating other trans people was as a nonbinary transperson. Shea is a trans guy, and loves to celebrate his queerness, which I also love. I finally found someone who absolutely accepts my nonbinary-ness without question — and I felt, for nonbinary and agender people like myself, that was rare. I finally feel like I'm enough as is, without changing my presentation to fit how I believe others will be attracted to me.

I'm also excluded in gendered bathroom usage. Very few places, restaurants including, have gender neutral or unisex bathrooms. My work is no exception: there, I begrudgingly use the women's bathroom, but I get in and out as fast as possible. I feel the need to avert the eyes of others in there, to duck my head down against their questioning gazes. As an agender individual who usually presents strongly along the masculine spectrum, I don't feel comfortable entering the women's room; I don't feel like I *look* like I belong there. That, and — to me — to use a gendered bathroom is to implicitly comply with the cisnormative assumption that there are *just two genders*. I would much rather use unisex or gender neutral bathrooms. Thus, in my gender variance, I don't feel accepted in the women's room. But in the same bathroom discussion vein, I don't feel I "pass" enough to use the men's bathroom in public. I'll only do so if it's a single stall men's bathroom.

I am excluded from my primary group of AFAB, cis-identifying females in that I don't ID as "female" or a "woman" or any of those such identities, yet I still have to engage with "female-bodied" dialogue: I still have a period, I don't intend to go on testosterone, and I feel obligated to use the women's bathroom in public. On the flip side and to the contrary, even though I *don't* identify with my AFAB designation, I feel that for those who do not know me on a personal level, I'm still not "trans enough," or "look trans enough," or am perceived as trans because I haven't changed my body with hormones. To live my genderfluid, agender, and trans experience is to constantly prove my identity through dialogue, written or otherwise, through personal essays and arguments.

Wouldn't it be grand if, without question, my nonbinary identities were accepted as is, without me having to constantly prove them against the roiling riptide of cisheteronormativity that seeks to squelch them? Yes, it would. But until that day arrives, I'm here to advocate for not only myself, but other agender, genderfluid, and all nonbinary folks out there. The road to overcoming forcible binarization is a long and lasting one, but I'm setting out on it nonetheless.

23: Virtually Myself
2017

I think it all started, as most things do, back in college. It's almost a stereotype to say that people went through experimental phases or "found themselves" in college, I know, but in my case, it's true. In my case, though, it happened in an entirely unexpected place... the internet.

I remember the day I first logged into the IRC channel (internet relay chat, what passed for chatrooms in those days) for the network of community colleges I was attending. I had to choose a username, and for want of something better, I pulled the first thing out of my mind: Kilroy. I had been getting into the band Styx for a few months, and it was a name I honestly liked. What I discovered about why I liked it and what it did for me, though, would change my entire outlook.

You see, for the very first time, people that I was speaking to saw my name and personality before they saw my face or heard my voice. For the first time, people judged me by what I said and how I said it, not by what was apparent physically on the surface. For the first time... people assumed I was male.

It wasn't a surprise to me that I liked this. I can't honestly say I "always knew" or that I felt like a boy from the time I was a very young child, because I really didn't. Some days I felt more girly, some days I definitely didn't, but as a child, I had a unique opportunity to be "just me" for the most part. I grew up amongst Barbie and Hot Wheels. I had dresses and pants. I ran around singing songs from the Marlo Thomas record I had as a child, content in the knowledge that it didn't matter if I was a boy or a girl. I wasn't too far into my teens, though, before I discovered that I was more than a little uncomfortable with the way my body was developing. I leaned more and more toward tomboyish behaviors. I clung to male role-models. I felt, underneath my problematic frame, that I was far more masculine than feminine. So, when people started "mistaking" me for male online, I did the predictable thing... I didn't correct anybody.

The results were far more telling than anything in my life had been to that point. I loved who I was able to become online. It was the first time I truly became a non-binary entity, able to jump out of my skin with all of its gendered baggage and into a world where I wasn't a boy or a girl, I was just vaguely masculine, just *me*. I discovered myself hiding from other people in the computer center, trying not to let it be known to anybody else who I was or where I was sitting. I didn't want to break the beautiful image I had created by letting myself be labeled as *female*. In cyberspace, I had found I was free to be who I truly was.

As times and technology advanced, it probably comes as no surprise that I kept finding new outlets with which to explore my identity. As a proud self-identified geek, I had already been playing tabletop role-playing games for years, and trying to deal with the frustration of playing predominantly male characters whilst inhabiting a body that didn't match. With the invention of MMORPGs, though, I found my true haven. There was a whole virtual world out there where I could walk around and interact with other players, and the body in which I did it was a simple matter of choosing the option I wanted.

I logged in online, and began to create not just a name and a set of abilities, but a body, a face, a full appearance that others playing the game would see. At last I had an avatar, a mechanism to avoid the unfortunate circumstance of playing yet another male character and having my well-meaning friends at the table continue to say "she" all the time. I presented myself as masculine, and I was received as masculine by my peers.

I was in heaven.

Before too long, though, I found myself having an entirely new issue that threw yet another wrench into an already complicated set of works: toxic masculine privilege. I've heard that a big part of privilege is not knowing that you have it. Once on the inside, I discovered it's not all sunshine and rainbows to finally be "one of the boys" when you've lived outside of that.

Men who didn't know I was sitting behind a keyboard in a body that required F to be stamped on my driver's license would make all sorts of comments about women that ranged from insensitive to outright offensive. Men who had no way to know that I had actually experienced menstruation would think it was okay to blame any behavior they saw as overly emotional on "that time of the month" if they knew the person they were ridiculing was female. Men would include me in all sorts of lewd private conversations about women without knowing that, were we to meet on the street face to face, they might be saying the same things about me.

Once again, I found myself hiding, afraid of being discovered if I called out the toxic behaviors, if I didn't play along with all of the hyper-masculine posturing. I remained silent then they said the things that infuriated me. I altered the things I typed so I sounded "tougher" or more straightforward, and I didn't use overly descriptive or flowery language. I tried to become "one of them" as best I could.

It was... weird. I felt awkward. I felt, yet again, like I was in the wrong place, like I didn't really fit. I had already discovered that even when dealing with polite gamers (of which there are many, in case this treatise cast all in a bad light due to the few) I felt amazing being called "he" or "him", yet words like "sir" and "man" still felt really awkward, almost too male for me in a way. It confused me that the people I should have felt most comfortable around were starting to feel less and less like who I was, who I wanted to be.

I guess what I'm saying is that the change in understanding who I was didn't happen overnight, even when I was finally able to slip into a male body and walk around a virtual universe. Inside, I didn't fit into one of those neat little boxes, my avatar didn't just come in the kind with broad shoulders or the kind with breasts. Over time, I found myself manipulating those sliders as much as I could... lowering the height, slimming the waists, looking for longer hair that would be programmed to fit on the male models, softening the angular faces. I worked, at times for hours, to create the perfect androgynous male bodies that I could pilot. The ones that would stand up for women gamers in the face of toxic masculinity. The ones that would make people second-guess whether to make that gay joke in my presence or not. The ones that looked, for all intents and purposes, to be just a little queer.

Over time, it worked. Given time to explore without the pressure that came with being constantly misgendered and harassed, I found my space, I found my identity, and I found myself. I was comfortable. I was free. Finally, I knew who I was. There was just one problem.

Eventually, I had to log off, and go back to real life.

That, I think was what finally prompted me to take action, to look into resources, and to finally come out and socially and medically transition. I was weary of the dual life, of having two sets of friends, of being afraid to introduce my friends on one server to players I knew face-to-face on another server, for fear the dreaded pronouns would slip in and break everything I had built.

(Also, it was exhausting to always find some new excuse for why I wasn't able to chat over a headset with programs like TeamSpeak!) I had to choose, and eventually, I chose to be me, and become in the flesh who I had become online, where I had no barriers, no walls, and no telling gender markers holding me back.

At this time I don't plan on any surgeries. I am on testosterone therapy, but I maintain a low dose. I sing in a men's choir, but I work carefully to develop my new voice in the tenor range. When I speak on the phone, it's a toss-up what pronouns and titles I get addressed with. My transition is still a process. I am changing my name, my gender marker, and my overall presentation to be seen out in the physical world as the masculine person I want to be... but in reality, I'm still there behind the keyboard, playing with the sliders, changing my hair, swapping clothes and taking measures to make sure I become the perfect queer avatar I have always known myself to be.

To Parents Everywhere

Just prior to this book going to print, there was a parent in a transgender and non-binary support group on Facebook who said their teenage child had just come out as non-binary to them, and they wanted some advice. One of the comments stood out above the rest, and it was written by none other than one of our contributors.

We are conveying that comment (with a few edits for clarity and with permission) to parents everywhere to read and reflect upon when and if their child comes to them and says they are non-binary. They may use another gender non-conforming term, including gender fluid, agender, trans, or any one of a number of others. Whatever the terminology, they are taking a huge step in sharing this with you.

Advice for all parents of gender non-conforming kids (No matter how old they are!)

Well, first off, don't panic. Your child identifies as non-binary, imagine how much trust they've put in you when they revealed this to you. This is wonderful. Be proud.

Non-binary is when a person does not fully (or not at all) identify as either gender. They're neither man or woman, or both in one. Some lean more towards the masculine side, some more towards the feminine side. Some are in the middle. But none wants to transition fully to the other gender. However, sometimes non-binary itself leads to the realization that they may be FTM (female to male) or MTF (male to female) In some cases it is a process of realizing their self. All are valid, no matter what path they chose.

You may encounter a lot of disbelief, and your child may have some hurtful encounters of ridicule and bullying due to the fact that non-binary individuals are still fighting to be accepted as 'real.' Sometimes those attacks come from all sides, including from the trans community, unfortunately.

Please be the support they need in such times. If they want a binder, take their hand and look around at the various binder companies, together. Nothing will make them happier but watching their parent taking an interest in their journey. If they do not want to go on Testosterone at this point, that's fine. But keep an open mind, they might change their decision later.

The best you can do right now, is take their hand and be genuinely interested in them. Support their decisions, if they aren't harmful to their self. Respect their pronouns and choice of name, fashion etc. I know it feels as if you're giving your child away much too early, but you really aren't. Keep in mind that your child has a hard and rocky road ahead of them and they will need you, your support and love to master it.

There will be tears, maybe even outbursts and depression. Make sure your child knows that you consider *their gender real and valid. If they know that they have their parent(s) behind them, ready to hold them, protect them and sometimes scold them (if necessary) but always support them, they will have a much easier time navigating life.*

You got this. I wish you all the luck in the world.

--Kai Yves Avery

Glossary

Androgynous: The quality exhibited by people who are difficult to identify as either clearly male or clearly female, and may have characteristics of both male and female. Some trans people whose genders cannot be classified as strictly male or strictly female call themselves androgynes. Also known as Androgyny.

AFAB: Assigned Female at Birth. It is the sex or gender that a doctor, midwife or other declares (or assigns) an newly birthed infant to be upon inspection of the genitals, and generally becomes one's legal gender/sex on birth certificates and other identification documents. This assignment is generally incorrect for non-binary and trans individuals.

Binary Gender System: A culturally defined code of acceptable behaviors which teach that there only two and only two distinct states of gender, men and women, who are masculine and feminine.

Bind/Binding: The process of flattening one's breasts to have a more masculine or flat appearing chest.

Cisgender: A term used by some to describe people who are not transgender. "Cis-" is a Latin prefix meaning "on the same side as," and is therefore an antonym of "trans-."

Coming Out: Announcing to your family, friends or work associates some previously known only to one's self aspect of one's sexual or gender identity.

Fluid(ity) / Gender Fluid / Genderfluid: Generally describes an identity that is a fluctuating mix of masculine, feminine and in-between.

FTM: A person who identifies as "female-to-male," meaning a person who was assigned female at birth, but identifies and lives as a male, and who may or may not medically transition with hormones or surgery. It is not claimed by all transmasculine individuals due to its binary connotations. Also, many do not believe they were ever "female," so there is no "transition" in the respect of female to male. It is a personal choice, and only to be used if that is how a person identifies.

Gender Expression / Presentation: How a person represents or expresses one's gender identity to others, often through behavior, clothing, hairstyles, voice or body characteristics.

Gender Identity: An individual's internal sense of being male, female, or something else. Since gender identity is internal, one's gender identity is not necessarily visible to others.

Gender Non-Conforming: A term used to describe some people whose gender expression is different from conventional expectations of masculinity and femininity. Not all gender non-conforming people identify as transgender; nor are all transgender people gender non-conforming. The term is not a synonym for transgender or transsexual and should only be used if someone self-identifies as gender non-conforming.

Gender Oppression: is the systemic manner in which certain groups are privileged or disadvantaged because of their gender. Intersects with discrimination based on race, sexuality, ability, class, age, history of incarceration, religion, language, and citizenship status. In other words, it is the societal, institutional, and individual beliefs and practices that privilege cisgender (gender-typical people, see "cisgender") and subordinate and disparage transgender, non-binary or gender variant people. Also known as "genderism."

Gender role: Describes the set of expectations that are ascribed to a certain gender in any given culture, relating to how to people of that gender "should" (among other things) behave, talk, dress, and think.

Genderqueer: A term used by some individuals who identify as neither entirely male nor entirely female. These are generally individuals who do not-- or will not -- adhere to the expectation of the only two gender presentations that which our culture allows.

Hormone Replacement Therapy: Medical treatment using hormones, used by some individuals to affect the development of secondary sex characteristics such as growing facial/body hair or lowering one's voice for those born AFAB. In non-transsexual individuals, the use of hormones is most-often used to treat the discomforts of menopause or to replace hormones (especially estrogen) lost after menopause.

HRT: See Hormone Replacement Therapy

Intersex: A term used for people who are born with a reproductive or sexual anatomy and/or chromosome pattern that does not seem to fit typical definitions of male or female.

Misogyny: the hatred and denigration of women and characteristics deemed feminine.

Non-binary: Non-binary people are those who don't feel 100% male or 100% female, no matter what sex/gender they were assigned at birth. They may feel like both or like something in between. They may have a gender that changes over time or they may not relate to gender at all.

Packer: A phallic device worn on the groin and under clothing for any purposes including: (for someone without a biological penis) the validation or confirmation of one's masculine gender identity; seduction; and/or sexual readiness (for one who likes to penetrate another during sexual intercourse).

Pansexual: A person who is sexually attracted to all or many gender expressions.

Pass: To be accepted without question in your chosen gender. The term has a problematic history and connotation, as some people believe that "passing" denotes a deception—a way of "fooling" others.

Queer: A term used to refer to lesbian, gay, bisexual and, often also transgender, people. Depending on the context, the term can be either a derogatory or affirming, as there are those in the LGBT community have sought to reclaim the term that was once widely used in a negative way. Not everyone agrees with its use or identifies with this term, but there many non-binary people who identify as queer.

Patriarchy: A system of society or government in which men hold the power and women are largely excluded from it.

Sexism: Discrimination based on gender, especially discrimination against women (including those perceived as women); the belief that one gender is superior to the other, especially that men are superior to women.

Stereotype: A preconceived or oversimplified generalization about an entire group of people without regard for their individual differences. Though often negative, can also be complimentary. Even positive stereotypes can have a negative impact, however, simply because they involve broad generalizations that ignore individual realities.

Testosterone (T): The hormone that is essential for the development of male characteristics, including muscle mass and strength, fat distribution, bone mass, facial hair growth, voice change and sex drive.

Third Gender: Someone who does not identify with the traditional genders of "man" or "woman" but identifies with another gender; it is a gender category available in some countries that recognize three or more genders.

Top Surgery: Top surgery refers to removal of the breasts to give a more masculine appearance. Also known as Chest Reconstruction Surgery.

Transgender: A term for people whose gender identity, expression or behavior is different from those typically associated with their assigned sex at birth. Transgender is a broad term and can cover transsexual people as well as non-binary people, if they so choose to identify as transgender.

Transmasculine: A term used to describe transgender people who were assigned female at birth, but identify with masculinity to a greater extent than with femininity.

Transphobia: Discrimination of and negative attitudes toward transgender people based on their gender expression.

Transition: The time when a person begins to living as the gender with which they identify rather than the gender they were assigned at birth, which often, but not always, includes changing one's name, and perhaps dressing or expressing their outward presentation differently. Transitioning may or may not also include medical and legal aspects, including taking hormones, having surgery, or changing identity documents (e.g. driver's license, Social Security record) to reflect one's gender identity.

Transsexual: An term which some people use whose

gender identity is different from their assigned sex at birth, and who seeks to physically transition from male to female or female to male. Not all are able to afford a medical transition. Many contemporary trans and non-binary people do not prefer this term, and it should never be used unless a person specifically tells you they identify as such.

.

References

Almodóvar, P. (2011). The Skin I live in. Warners Espana

Althusser, L. (2014). *On the Reproduction of Capitalism Ideology and Ideological State Apparatuses*. London: Verso

Baum, L. F., & Neill, J. R. (2000). *The Marvelous Land of Oz: Being an Account of the Further Adventures of the Scarecrow and Tim Woodman..., a Sequel to the Wizard of Oz*. University of Virginia Library.

Bornstein, K (1998) *My Gender Workbook: How to Become a Real Man, a Real Woman, the Real You, Or Something Else Entirely*. New York and London: Routledge.

Bornstein, K., & Bergman, S. B. (2010). *Gender Outlaws: The Next Generation*. Berkeley, CA: Seal Press.

Butler, J. (1988). Performative acts and gender constitution: An essay in phenomenology and Feminist Theory. *Theatre Journal, 40*(4), 519–531. http://doi.org/10.2307/3207893.

Carver, P.R., Yunger, J.L., & Perry, D.G. (2003). Gender identity and adjustment in middle childhood. *Sex Roles, 49*(3/4), 95–109. http://dx.doi.org/10.1023/A:1024423012063

Clarke-Billings, L. (2016, November 18). What do Tinder's 37 new gender identity options mean? *Newsweek*. Retrieved from http://www.newsweek.com/what-do-tinders-37-new-gender-identity-options-mean-522679

Cohen-Kettenis, P.T., Owen, A., Kaijser, V.G., Bradley, S.J., & Zucker, K.J. (2003). Demographic characteristics, social competence, and behavior problems in children with gender identity disorder: a cross-national, cross-clinic comparative analysis. *Journal of Abnormal Child Psychology, 31*(1), 41–53. http://dx.doi.org/10.1023/A:1021769215342

Cohen, P. N. (2015). *The Family: Diversity, Inequality, and Social Change.* New York: W.W. Norton & Company.

Coleman, E., Bockting, W., Botzer, M., Cohen-Kettenis, P., DeCuypere, G., Feldman, J., ... & Monstrey, S. (2012). Standards of care for the health of transsexual, transgender, and gender-nonconforming people, version 7. *International journal of transgenderism, 13*(4), 165-232.

Corrine, C. (2018, April 5). No more her, she, her, him. Colleges use gender neutral pronouns. *Cat Country 107.3 WPUR.* Retrieved from http://catcountry1073.com/no-more-her-she-her-him-colleges-use-gender-neutral-pronouns/

Creighton, S. (2001). Surgery for intersex. *Journal of the Royal Society of Medicine, 94*(5), 218-220.

Day Walker. (2016). Waiting for the third line. In M.E. Brown (Ed.) *The Herstory of Transmasculine Identities: An Annotated Anthology.* (pp. 137-140). Miami, FL: Boundless Endeavors.

Deaux, K., & Lewis, L. L. (1984). Structure of gender stereotypes: Interrelationships among components and gender label. *Journal Of Personality And Social Psychology, 46*(5), 991-1004. doi:10.1037/0022-3514.46.5.991

Devor, H. (1989). *Gender Blending: Confronting the Limits of Duality* (Vol. 533). Bloomington, IN: Indiana University Press.

Ellemers, N. (2018). Gender stereotypes. *Annual review of psychology, 69.*

Endendijk, J. J., Derks, B., & Mesman, J. (2018). Does parenthood change implicit gender-role stereotypes and ehaviors?. *Journal of Marriage and Family, 80*(1), 61-79.

Facebook Diversity. (2018). Facebook.com. Retrieved from https://www.facebook.com/ facebookdiversity/posts/774221582674346)

Fanon, F. (1967). *Black Skin White Masks.* New York, New York: Grove Press, Inc.

Fanon, F. (2000). The Fact of Blackness. In L.Back & J. Solmos (Eds.), *Theories of Race and Racism: A Reader.* (pp. 257-266) New York, Routledge.

Feinberg, L. (1998). *Trans Liberation: Beyond Pink or Blue.* Boston, MA: Beacon.

Feinberg, L. (2003). Transgender liberation: A movement whose time has come. In C.R. McCann & S-K Kim (Authors), *Feminist Theory Reader: Local and Global Perspectives.* (pp. 148-58). New York: Routledge.

Gartner, R. E., & Sterzing, P. R. (2018). Social ecological correlates of family-level interpersonal and environmental microaggressions toward sexual and gender minority adolescents. *Journal of Family Violence, 33*(1), 1-16.

Glick, P., & Fiske, S. T. (2001). An ambivalent alliance: Hostile and benevolent sexism as complementary justifications for gender inequality. *American Psychologist, 56*(2), 109.

Harrison, J., Grant, J., & Herman, J. L. (2011). A gender not listed here: Genderqueers, gender rebels, and Otherwise in the National Transgender Discrimination Survey. *LGBTQ Policy Journal, 213.*

Haynes, F., & McKenna, T. (Eds.). (2001). *Unseen genders: Beyond the binaries* (Vol. 12). Peter Lang Pub Incorporated.

Hemmings, C. (2012). Affective solidarity: Feminist reflexivity and political transformation. *Feminist Theory, 13*(2), 147-161.

Hillary, A. (2014). On the erasure of queer autistic people. In C. Wood (Ed.), *Criptiques* (pp. 121-146). May Day.

Intons-Peterson, M. J., & Reddel, M. (1984). What do people ask about a neonate? *Developmental Psychology, 20,* 358-359.

Jack, J. (2012). Gender copia: Feminist rhetorical perspectives on an autistic concept of sex/gender. *Women's Studies in Communication, 35*(1), 1-17.

Karraker, K. H., Vogel, D. A., & Lake, M. A. (1995). Parents' gender-stereotyped perceptions of newborns: The eye of the beholder revisited. *Sex Roles, 33*(9-10), 687-701.

Lee, E. E., & Troop-Gordon, W. (2011). Peer socialization of masculinity and femininity: Differential effects of overt and relational forms of peer victimization. *British Journal Of Developmental Psychology, 29*(2), 197-213. doi:10.1111/j.2044-835X2010.02022.x

Levitt, H. M., & Hiestand, K. R. (2004). A quest for authenticity: Contemporary butch gender. *Sex Roles, 50*(9-10), 605-621.

LoBue, V., & DeLoache, J. S. (2011). Pretty in pink: The early development of gender-stereotyped colour preferences. *British Journal of Developmental Psychology, 29*(3), 656-667.

Lorde, A. (1984). Uses of the erotic: The erotic as power. *Sister Outsider: Essays and Speeches.* (pp. 53-59). Trumansburg, NY: Crossing.

Martin, C. L., Ruble, D. N., & Szkrybalo, J. (2002). Cognitive theories of early gender development. *Psychological bulletin, 128*(6), 903. doi:10.1037/0033-2909.128.6.903. Money, J., Hampson, J. G., & Hampson, J. L. (1955). An examination of some basic sexual concepts: the evidence of human hermaphroditism. *Bulletin of the Johns Hopkins Hospital, 97*(4), 301.

Meerkamper, S.T. (2014). Non-binary identities & the law. *Transgender Law Center.* Retrieved from https://transgenderlawcenter.org/archives/10208

Merriam-Webster (2018). We added a gender-neutral pronoun in 1934. Why have so few people heard of it? *Merriam-Webster, Incorporated.* Retrieved from https://www.merriam-webster.com/words-at-play/third-person-gender-neutral-pronoun-thon

Mikkola, M. (2016). "Feminist perspectives on sex and gender", in *The Stanford Encyclopedia of Philosophy,* Zalta, E.N. (Ed). Retrieved from http://plato.stanford.edu/archives/fall2012/entries/feminismgender/.

Mizock, L., Mougianis, E., Meier, C., & Moundas, S. (2015). Gender diversity and transgender identity in youth. *Journal of Sexual Medicine, 5,* 1892-1897.

Muñoz, J.E. (1999). *Disidentifications: Queers of Color and the Performance of Politics.* Minneapolis: University of Minnesota,

Nicholson, L. (1994). Interpreting Gender. *Signs,* 79–105.

Olson, K. R., Key, A. C., & Eaton, N. R. (2015). Gender cognition in transgender children. *Psychological Science, 26*(4), 467-474. doi:10.1177/09567976 14568156

Perez, M. (2017, November 10). "Ladies" and "Gentlemen" banned by NYC Transit". *Newsweek*. Retrieved from http://www.newsweek.com/men-and-women-no-longer-exist-according-nyc-subways-708252

Prewitt-Freilino, J. L., Caswell, T. A., & Laakso, E. K. (2012). The gendering of language: A comparison of gender equality in countries with gendered, natural gender, and genderless languages. *Sex Roles, 66*(3-4), 268-281.

Rands, K. E. (2009). Considering Transgender People in Education: A gender-complex approach. *Journal of Teacher Education, 60*(4), 419-431.

Roberts, A.L., Rosario, M., Corliss, H.L., Koenen, K.C., & Austin, S.B. (2012). Childhood gender nonconformity: a risk indicator for childhood abuse and posttraumatic stress in youth. *Pediatrics, 129*(3), 410–417. http://dx.doi.org/10.1542/peds.2011-1804

Robinson, M. J. (2014). *Transgender inclusion in the workplace* (Doctoral dissertation, Cleveland State University).

Schifter, J. & Madrigal, J. (2000). *The Sexual Construction of Latino Youth: Implications For the Spread of HIV/AIDS*. New York: The Haworth Hispanic/Latino Press.

Serano, J. (2013). Trans woman manifesto. In W. Kolmar & F. Bartkowski (Eds.) *Feminist Theory: A Reader*, (pp. 547-551). New York, NY: McGraw-Hill

Shepard, D. S., Gurewich, D., Lwin, A. K., Reed, G. A., & Silverman, M. M. (2016). Suicide and suicidal attempts in the United States: costs and policy implications. *Suicide and life-threatening behavior*, 46(3), 352-362.

Skorinko, J. L. M. (2018). Riddle Me This: Using Riddles That Violate Gender Stereotypes To Demonstrate The Pervasiveness Of Stereotypes. *Psychology Learning & Teaching*, 1475725717752181.

Steinmetz, K. (2017, March 16). Beyond 'He' or 'She': The Changing Meaning of Gender and Sexuality. *Time, Inc.* Retrieved from http://time.com/magazine/southpacific/4703711/ march-27th-2017-vol-189-no-11-asia-europe-middle-east-and-africa-south-pacific/

Stoller, R. J. (1968) *Sex and Gender: On The Development of Masculinity and Femininity.* New York: Science House.

strangeloved. (n.d.). Queer as Cat. Retrieved June 17, 2017 from queerascat.tumblr.com/post/91654136619/strangegloved-ok-so-the-rly-cool-people-at-the,

Stryker, S. (2008). *Transgender History.* Seal Press.

Sullivan, T. S. (2017). *Conversion therapy ground zero: Interrogating the production of gender as a pathology in the United States.* A Dissertation Submitted to the Faculty of the California Institute of Integral Studies in Partial Fulfillment of the Requirements for the Degree of Doctor of Philosophy Social and Cultural Anthropology

Thompson, A. J. (2014). Linguistic relativity: Can gendered languages predict sexist attitudes? *Linguistics, Montclair State University.*

Transtistic. (n.d.). What is Gendervague? MOGAI Lexi-
con. Retrieved June 17, 2017 from https://tran-
stistic.wordpress.com/2017/06/17/what-is-gen-
dervague/

Veale, J., Saewyc, E., Frohard-Dourlent, H., Dobson, S.,
Clark, B. & the Canadian Trans Youth Health Sur-
vey Research Group. (2015). *Being Safe, Being Me:
Results of the Canadian Trans Youth Health Survey.*
Vancouver, BC: Stigma and Resilience Among
Vulnerable Youth Centre, School of Nursing, Uni-
versity of British Columbia. Retrieved from
https://saravyc.sites.
olt.ubc.ca/files/2015/05/SARAVYC_Trans-
Youth-Health-Report_EN_Final_Web2.pdf

West, C., & Zimmerman, D. H. (1987). Doing gender. *Gender & society, 1*(2), 125-151.

UK Trans Info. (2015). Non-binary experiences of
healthcare. *Action for Trans* Health.*
http://uktrans.info/research/45-medical-re-
search/378-experiences-of-non-binary-people-
accessing-healthcare

Wilchins R (2004b) *Queer Theory, Gender Theory: An Instant Primer.* Los Angeles, CA: Alyson Books

About the Editors

Michael Eric Brown is the Founding Executive Director of TransMentors International, Inc., a non-profit organization dedicated to supporting trans and non-binary individuals in their day-to-day lives. He is known for his contributions both on and offline, especially in the realm of social justice and gender concerns.

A scholar who is interested in how people's thoughts, feelings, and behaviors are influenced by the actual, imagined, or implied presence of others, Michael is working his way towards a PhD in Social Psychology in order to provide vital research on the lives of trans and non-binary individuals. As a professional freelance writer, he writes on a variety of subjects and engages his readers with his unique writing style. He has published a number of books on the transmasculine experience as well as other subjects

Daywalker Burill was born in 1965 in Oakland, California. Their focus on Behavioral Psychology has enabled them to provide deep insights into the transgender and Butch-Femme communities through their writing as well as gender related discussion on platforms such as forums, social media groups and conference panel discussions. For over 20 years they have been an active participant and Mentor in the Butch Femme Community promoting the dynamics of diversity and the spirit of inclusion within the Culture.

Daywalker is Agender and now resides in Northern California with their wife after having spent much of their career meandering through the Motorcycle industry. They have been described as a Hippy, a Modern day Philosopher, a Peace maker, a reflective Author, an Artist of the Fluorescence, and a Gender anomalous.

More Books by Michael Eric Brown

You can find these books and more at www. BoundlessEndeavors.com

The Herstory of Transmasculine Identities
Copyright© 2016. Michael Eric Brown
ISBN: 978-0-9968309-2-8

Unravelling the complex intersections of FTM gender transitions, lesbianism and feminism... Identities. Gender concerns. Misogyny. Objectification. Politics. Patriarchy. Discrimination. Rejection. Losses. Gains. Emotions.

Part One explores the deeper meanings, definitions and embodiments of gender, sexuality, and identity, including the social and personal politics of each. Part Two contains the stories and experiences of individuals who welcome this opportunity to share their lives in order to facilitate understanding, acceptance and education.

This book, which is being used by educators nationwide, shares stories of those individuals who came from the lesbian community and how they arrived at the place they are now in their identities. There are also stories from those who were not a part of the lesbian community but adhered to a strong feminist perspective, having to overcome reservations of moving from a gender associated with oppression to one associated with privilege. These stories encompass a variety of experiences with exploring gender, sexuality, and identity.

Pencil Me In: A Trans Perspective in a Gendered World
Copyright© 2015 Michael Eric Brown
ISBN: 978-0-9968309-0-4

Michael Eric Brown shares not only his personal life as a transgender man, but he also talks candidly about gender roles and societal expectations. Approaching the subjects with frankness and occasional humor, he shares his experiences as well as those of countless others in the transgender community in order to communicate openly what it means to be a transgender individual in today's society. This book presents a straight-forward examination of definitions and perceptions of gender roles and expectations, and the oppression transgender people are forced to overcome due to these expectations. Covering areas such as the language of gender, feminist views, oppression and more, Michael approaches the subject of being transgender in a world that is still struggling to acknowledge that gender really isn't just a black and white binary concept. He applies personal examples, observations and statistics in order to enlighten and educate in an informative and reader-friendly style.

Defining Myself: Transmasculine Experience Through Poetry

The collective works of thirty-eight individuals who have revealed their deepest emotions in written word. Over seventy poems putting a voice to the process of living authentically in one's gender. Words which have come from the depths of their beings—from the ache of depression, the fiery pits of anger, darkness of their fears, and the deep wells of loss; as well as from their journeys of change to their passions of joy and acceptance.

All are transmasculine, meaning they identify somewhere on the masculine side of the gender spectrum. Some may be fully transitioned female-to-male (FTM) while others may be non-binary, gender fluid or simply transmasculine, with or without having gone through a physical transition. It is not the physical that makes the person—it is the self-identification, the self-love and self-acceptance—and it is all these experiences in each of these individuals that help create our diverse community of transmasculine folks.

Made in the USA
Las Vegas, NV
29 April 2021